D1438690

Text and photographs
Copyright (C) Police Mutual Assurance Society
First published in Great Britain, 1992
by
Police Mutual Assurance Society
Alexandra House, Queen Street,
Lichfield, Staffordshire

ISBN No 0 9518996 0 0

Printed by Craft Print Pte Ltd Singapore

THE STORY OF THE
POLICE
MUTUAL
ASSURANCE
SOCIETY
■ PETER N. WALKER ■

Police Mutual Assurance Society,
Alexandra House, Queen Street,
Lichfield, Staffs.

The compilation and production of this book has been a team effort and I wish to thank the Chairman and Committee of Management of the PMAS for their support at all stages. Particular thanks go to Mr Peter Sharpe, the General Manager, his secretary Gill Bird and many other members of the administrative staff at Alexandra House, Lichfield for their friendly but highly professional assistance with my research.

With regard to the production of the book, I would also like to record my appreciation for the assistance given by Publishing Consultant, Lesley Hadcroft (a former woman police constable and PMAS member) of Laurence Pollinger Limited, 18, Maddox Street, London W1R OEU, Martin Kerr of The Pinpoint Design Company, Linslade, Leighton Buzzard, Bedfordshire, David Ward of David Bruce Graphics Ltd, Plaistow, London E13, Andrew Rosso of Craft Print (Europe) Ltd, Newbury, Berkshire and indexer Christopher Norris.

Their contribution towards the publication of this book has been of the highest possible standard.

PETER N. WALKER

The illustrations on pages 10, 78 and the cover of the book *The Policeman* (1962) on page 76 are from original paintings by John Berry and are reproduced by kind permission of Ladybird Books Ltd.

Also, a number of photographs which appear throughout the book are reproduced by kind permission of the Lichfield Mercury and The Wolverhampton Express and Star.

CONTENTS

INTRODUCTION

Mr Peter J. Sharpe, FCII, General Manager

Anyone reading "The Story of the PMAS" can be left in no doubt as to the resolve of the police to serve their colleagues through the medium of their very own Mutual Assurance Society.

Over the years, a remarkable range of characters has served the PMAS, men and women of true steel; and a list of the office holders almost reads like a *"Who's Who"* of the British Police Service. The problems of starting, nurturing and directing the Police Mutual against a background of fundamental change in social attitudes and in the police service itself, plus a wealth of legislation affecting and changing our financial institutions, would at times have deterred fainter hearts.

But those connected with the Police Mutual down the years were determined to overcome every problem in their continuing aim to serve their colleagues and their families through their very own assurance society. Many who, in their generation, have contributed to the success of the PMAS are mentioned in Peter Walker's book. Regrettably but inevitably many more are not − there is just not the space to refer to all in the manner they deserve. But the Society owes a huge debt to all those who have, in their different ways, helped it along the road to such success by their selfless and individual contributions.

The list includes Committee members, authorised officers, executive and staff, and professional associates − all have been infected with that unique PMAS spirit and have combined to use their special talents in the interests of the Society and its members.

The commitment of those involved with the PMAS often comes as a surprise to many who are not familiar with the Society's operations. In contrast to many organisations, successive

Presidents have unfailingly demonstrated a practical interest in the work of the Society, as well as their concern for its members and the well-being of those who serve them.

Over the years, the balance of responsibility within the overall PMAS team has altered, for although the fundamental objective of the Society has not changed, the environment in which the work of the Society is conducted certainly has. Successive Chairmen, in particular, have demonstrated fine judgement in helping to ensure these changes have taken place in an orderly and prudent manner. The result is that the Society is enabled to be professionally and positively managed while being directed by representatives of its police membership. Within this team, police and financial professionals work together in an atmosphere of mutual respect and with resolute commitment.

This book is evidence of how those virtues have, in the past, served the police through their own Society. As the pace of the world quickens, it also reminds us of the nature of our heritage and provides some useful pointers for the future.

FOREWORD

Sir John Woodcock, CBE, QPM, CBIM
HM Chief Inspector of Constabulary
President of the Police Mutual
Assurance Society

It gives me great pleasure to write the foreword to "The Story of the PMAS", a Society in which the police service takes great pride.

To look back on the achievement of its 70 years is tremendously interesting. From such small beginnings it has grown and expanded until it is the flourishing Society it is today.

Looking at the limits of cover in earlier days it is hard to believe just what feelings of comfort and security it gave to serving police officers. Indeed, the ten shillings (50p) a week for a thousand pounds cover, plus profits, in the early 1950s, for example, was not easily found! All things are comparative, and the young constable then felt the same confidence that his family was provided for as the present day officer.

Talking as I do to so many police officers, it emerges that, whatever the financial climate, we know that our Society will perform as well as the best.

Perhaps the most outstanding feature of dealing with the PMAS is that, whether you talk to your force representative or whether you take your problem to the General Manager himself, you are assured of a courteous and caring service. Personal attention is always given to your particular difficulties and you are left with a feeling that nothing has been spared to provide an answer. If ever there was an example of quality of service, it is here. If every police officer dealt with every problem and every enquiry in the same caring way, it would go a long way to eliminating many complaints.

The production of this history in such an imaginative way is an illustration of your confidence and pride in your achievements. I am proud to be the President of the Society which I joined in the early 1950s. I am sure it will continue to go from strength to strength.

Illustration from Ladybird Book 'The Policeman'. Originals from this book were acquired by the Society in 1990 and hang in the boardroom at Alexandra House, Lichfield. The artist John Berry is represented in the Imperial War Museum.

CHAPTER 1

IN THE BEGINNING

The Police Mutual Assurance Association
1866 – 1921

The remarkable story of the Police Mutual Assurance Society would be incomplete without an account of the 19th century Association from which it emerged. Together they span more than 125 years in the history of both the police service and of police mutual assurance.

That early organisation was the Police Mutual Assurance Association which bears astonishing similarities to that of the Police Mutual Assurance Society – both made use of the voluntary services of authorised officers, both held annual meetings at different venues throughout the country, both had HMIs as their Presidents and senior police officers as chairmen of their Committees of Management, both were known as 'the Police Mutual', both served all ranks of the service, both had strong links with Birmingham and the Midlands, both won the services of long-term voluntary supporters of high police rank, both faced the problems of a world war and a major human disease, both faced decisions on how to expand and change to meet the increasing demands of an advanced and more sophisticated membership. And, of course, both were unique in their time because they were controlled by police officers solely for the benefit of police officers, their families and dependants.

An examination of the history of the old PMAA therefore produces some astonishing parallels with the PMAS which was its logical, natural and highly efficient successor. In terms of family relationships, the parent PMAA would have been extraordinarily proud of its offspring, the PMAS.

But who, precisely, can be regarded as the founder of the Police Mutual? The answer remains an intriguing mystery because the idea was propounded in a magazine called *The Police Service Advertiser* by someone writing under the pseudonym of 'Verdad'. He proposed the establishment of a mutual assurance scheme whereby a penny subscription would be paid upon the death of a brother-officer; that penny would be paid by *all* officers of the police forces of England and Wales irrespective of rank; the income would be for the benefit of the widow and/or family of the deceased officer if married, or a widower with a family, or for the benefit of a nominee of single officers.

The editor of *The Police Service Advertiser*, Mr T.F. Molyneux, recognised the merits of this proposal and urged a meeting to discuss the suggestion. He wrote to several senior officers and it was through his efforts that this important first meeting took place. On Monday 13th August 1866, therefore, a dozen police officers met at Windsor Police Station to discuss the creation of a police mutual assurance scheme.

For the record, they were: Deputy Chief Constable Maxwell (Exeter), Deputy Chief Constable Stretten (Cambridgeshire), Deputy Chief Constable Marson, (Huntingdonshire), Mr Gibson, Chief Clerk (Winchester Police), Mr Superintendent Young (Woburn, Bedfordshire), Mr Superintendent Goldsmith (Taunton, Somerset), Mr Superintendent Hodgkinson (Slough, Buckinghamshire), Mr Superintendent Grant (Reading, Berkshire), Mr Superintendent Long (Linton, Cambridgeshire), Head Constable Edgar (Windsor), Head Constable Rogers (Reigate) and Mr Inspector Reece of Berkshire. Head Constable was the name given to the most senior police officer in a borough force, some of which consisted of very few constables, as low as two in some cases; the counties had their chief constables, and it is interesting to see the courtesy title of 'Mr' which precedes the ranks of superintendent and inspector. This was not used in the case of sergeants and constables.

As the meeting opened, Mr Gibson was in a highly eloquent mood and delivered a long, emotional and somewhat flowery speech in which he praised the police and worried about their dependants if they died. He said, "We must remember that we are the representatives of thousands of fellow men, and that we have, although self-imposed, an important and sacred duty to perform."

With such noble sentiments and such fine language to encourage them, the meeting elected Mr Maxwell as chairman, and then Mr Gibson lost no time in moving that 'Verdad's' proposal be accepted. Superintendent Hodgkinson suggested the scheme be extended to Scotland and Ireland and it was Superintendent Young who put forward an alternative suggestion that different subscription rates be paid by different ranks.

'Verdad's' initial scheme was that all ranks should each pay one penny upon the death of a colleague, but that idea was soon changed to one with subscriptions that varied according to the rank of the member. At that time, the British currency comprised pounds, shillings and pence (£.s.d.) and there were 240 pennies to the £1 with 12 pennies to a shilling. A constable's wage was around 19 shillings (95p) per week. It had been calculated that if every constable and sergeant in the country paid just one penny, it would result in about £60 for the benefit of any dependants – that may seem a small sum now, but at that time it was more than a year's income for many.

The amended idea, which was later to be changed several more times, was that Inspectors, Superintendents and Head Constables would each pay half a crown (2s. 6d – 12½p) which would realise something around £70. 15s. 0d. (£70. 75) for the dependants of a brother officer. Sergeants and constables would continue to pay one penny which would realise about £60.

These proposals sounded fine, but they were perhaps just a little too ambitious because they were based on the assumption that every police officer in Britain would subscribe to the new association. To persuade everyone that it was a good idea would prove to be a huge undertaking but if only 50% of them joined, the returns would be worthwhile.

Flushed with idealism, however, the meeting decided that the *Police Service Advertiser* should maintain a list of everyone who wished to join the scheme, together with the names of the nominees who would receive the monies upon their death. It was also decided that an announcement of a death in that magazine would be sufficient proof of that fact.

Circulars would be sent to every police force suggesting that all forces become subscribers of the magazine, asking that they ensure the magazine was read by every officer, and inviting their comments upon the scheme. The meeting suggested that, upon the announcement of a death, the money due would be collected in each police force and sent, within six weeks of the death, to the Chief Constable or Head Constable of the force in which the deceased had served. That senior officer would then hand the monies to the nominees or a legal representative of the deceased, after expenses for postage and other administrative costs had been deducted. The money would be sent by Post Office order or money order, hopefully at a reduced rate.

It was a simple plan and the meeting was determined that the entire procedure would remain simple and very easy to administer. The question of simplicity arose when it was suggested that women be allowed to join, the women in question being the widows of deceased police officers. Mr Gibson maintained there could be no objection to this, provided it did not add complications to the overall scheme.

Superintendent Young said that the work involved in collecting and distributing the money should be done 'for the love of the thing'; when the meeting raised the question of appointing a secretary, he added that the secretary should likewise not receive any salary. "If nobody is willing to do it," said the worthy Superintendent, "I'll do it myself!". He was therefore the first secretary of the PMAA or the 'Police Mutual' as it became known.

The meeting heard a letter from General Cartwright who was one of Her Majesty's Inspector Generals of Constabulary; he said he would assist in any way he could and further support was promised by two more HMIs, Captain Willis and Colonel Woodford. The support of the country's HMIs, and its Chief HMIs when they were established in 1963, has always been a constant source of encouragement for the PMAA and the PMAS. In the minds of many officers, their endorsement of the Society provided the necessary air of authority and trustworthiness of the schemes.

Superintendent Young added that perhaps the HMIs could exert pressure on the Home Office to persuade the Post Office to ease their charges on the money orders which would be used. We do not know whether this was ever raised at the Home Office!

With the framework of the new Association agreed upon, it was decided to adjourn that first meeting so that work could begin upon formulation of the rules and procedures. Another meeting would be held in November, 1866, at which the formal rules would be presented for approval.

By 22nd November, 1866 those rules had been thoroughly discussed and altered slightly. Rule 1 was important and very specific because it said, "That the members of every constabulary and police force in England and Wales be invited to become members of the Association". Rule 2 said that every candidate on joining the force *will* be invited to join! There was no compulsion to join, but the rule clearly embraced all ranks. There was provision for officers leaving the force to remain members, whether they had retired or resigned, or had been required to resign through ill-health or injury. The rules added that every member would receive a copy of the rules, free of charge.

Among the modest changes to the rules which had been originally proposed was that instead of *The Police Service Advertiser* maintaining a list of members, every police force would compile its own list of members and nominees; in this way, branches of the

Association would be created. Nonetheless, a notice of the death of a member would be published in *The Police Service Advertiser* within a week of the death. When that notice appeared, every police force would, upon the first pay day thereafter, collect the amounts due.

In fact, the wording of that rule was perhaps a prediction of the system of deducting premiums from pay which was later to be adopted by the PMAS, because Rule 11 said, "On the first pay day after the publication of such notice (of death), the amount of subscriptions named in Rule 9 shall be stopped from the pay of every member of the association and transmitted by Post Office order to the force in which the officer was serving at the time of his death." Did this imply that members, even at that time, agreed to allow their subscriptions to be taken from their pay *before* they had received it? That is the current system used by the PMAS, but in fact most officers at that time handed over the necessary cash as they paraded on pay days to collect their wages. The authorised officer was on hand to make sure they handed over any PMAA subscriptions which had become due.

Those subscriptions, detailed in Rule 9, said that *every* member should pay one penny but those holding the ranks of Head Constable, Superintendent and Inspector must pay an additional 2s. 5d, thus making a total of 2s. 6d. That sum was known as half a crown at that time and so this list of members became known as the Half Crown List. A half crown comprised 30 pennies.

All Chief Constables and Head Constables were expected to become members as an example to their men. At that stage, there was no separate subscription for sergeants – they paid one penny. And there were no chief superintendent or chief inspector ranks at that time.

It was also the duty of the local Chief Constable or Head Constable to collect subscriptions from pensioners and others who had left the force. This was not an easy task but the rules stipulated that it should be done within one month of a member's death. The resultant monies, less expenses for postage and the cost of Post Office orders, would be sent to the Chief Constable of the deceased's force for handing to his dependants at the earliest opportunity. No expenses, other than the costs of transmission of the money, were permitted.

Even as these rules were being discussed, news was received of the death of PC Roberts and his wife in Carnarvonshire, both having died of cholera. PC Roberts had in fact attended the very first meeting of the Association in his own force and had indicated his intention to become a member. He had died before his intention became a reality. The meeting decided that an immediate enquiry would be launched to see if any dependants were left and, if so, the new PMAA would originate a subscription on behalf of that family. It was an amazing gesture of goodwill at such an early stage of the PMAA. In fact, it backfired.

The couple had no children, and so the dead constable's mother claimed the money because she claimed she was 'poor and next-of-kin'. But her claim was disallowed as she was neither a widow nor a nominee. The Association had been established, albeit six months after the constable's death, for the benefit of widows or nominees, not next-of-kin, however worthy they might be.

The first annual meeting of the PMAA was held in the Council Chamber at Birmingham on 19th August 1867. The President was Admiral Davies, Chief Constable of Cambridgeshire and Huntingdonshire, with Mr George Glossop, Head Constable of Birmingham as his Vice President. The Chairman of the Committee was Mr John Maxwell, Deputy Chief Constable of Devonshire. The Committee members were: Charles Stretten, DCC of Cambridgeshire, Captain Sylvester, Head Constable of Salford, Henry Hilton, Head Constable of Derby, Mr Bloxham, DCC of Somersetshire, Captain Henry Hilliker, a Superintendent from Devonshire, Mr M. Power, Head Constable of Worcester, Mr Allison, the Head Constable of Swansea and Mr Superintendent W. R. Young, the Superintendent from Bedfordshire who was the Association's first secretary, then an honorary post.

By this time, the rules had been modified in the light of experience already gained. One interesting fact is a change of wording which related to the collection of monies – wherever the word 'Chief Constable' or 'Head Constable' appeared, it should be replaced with the term 'Authorised Officer'.

Thus this new title came into being and it was the authorised officer's duty to collect subscriptions from members within his force and so the term was first used. Authorised officers have been responsible for the collection of PMAA and PMAS subscriptions ever since.

Among the other decisions taken at Birmingham was one which established that the annual meeting be located at different places throughout Britain during August. This was done so that as many forces and as many police officers as possible could become acquainted with the Association by attending these meetings.

Scottish police forces were admitted too, and the first balance sheet was published. An appeal for monies to fund those first weeks produced a vital £22. 10s. 0d (£22. 50) and during the year, this was used for printing, postage and the issue of circulars. After expenditure, the balance was £4. 0s. 9d. which is £4. 04 in current monetary terms. During 1867, there had been 15 deaths from which dependants had received money donated by police officers throughout the nation, and so the infant PMAA was already proving its worth. News of its admirable purpose quickly spread among police forces and very soon, the PMAA had over 2,000 members throughout the police forces of Britain.

But its inexperience was already causing problems. One was the delay in collecting subscriptions; in one case, almost four months elapsed between the death of the policeman and the date the money was passed to his widow; three months was not unusual and so the Association urged its authorised officers to do their best to be prompt in this urgent and somewhat distressing matter.

The shortest time was a matter of five weeks or so, and the system would not allow payment of the monies to the recipients until literally every penny had been collected. There were no part payments and no advances of any kind.

Further problems were arising from the two lists of subscribers, the penny list and the half-crown list. At the August 1868 annual meeting in Bath, the committee heard that in two cases, officers had been paying 2s. 6d when in fact they were listed as sergeants when they died, thus their dependants were receiving income from penny subscriptions. It transpired that they were Inspectors of Nuisances in their boroughs and had therefore regarded themselves as Inspectors for Association purposes. And they had paid their half-crown when colleagues had died.

These claims were honoured, but the Association was learning that it must exercise care and control over its members and its funds. One member even suggested the payment of subscriptions in advance, so that a small reserve fund would be created.

Just one advance payment would be necessary to establish a small reserve of cash and this would aid the beneficiaries because they would receive prompt payments; it would also ease the burden of the authorised officers in having more time to collect cash from all their scattered members. But the notion was rejected; police officers were very wary of paying for anything in advance and they failed to understand the merits of that proposal.

The Committee decided that there should be more lists and produced the idea of a 1st class list for Superintendents and above who would pay 2s.6d; a 2nd class list for Inspectors who would pay two shillings; a 3rd class list for Sergeants who would pay threepence and a 4th class list for Constables who would continue to pay one penny.

At that 1868 meeting, one committee member suggested that the widows of police officers be admitted to the Association so that, in the event of their death, they would not suffer a pauper's burial and any children would benefit. It was suggested too, that

19

the wife of a serving officer might become a member. Both suggestions were rejected, chiefly due to the problems of collecting subscriptions – the hard-worked authorised officers were already having enormous problems collecting from their colleagues. In two cases, officers absconded with the takings, and several police forces were in arrears – one was Windsor, the host force for the foundation meeting.

In order to encourage forces to pay their subscriptions on time, entire police forces were threatened with expulsion from the Association if they were in serious arrears. Six weeks was considered the longest time required to make a full collection.

In 1870, the borough force of Richmond in Yorkshire was expelled – it had only two constables and neither bothered to pay his dues, and then Windsor was struck off the register for non-payment of its subscriptions. In another case, a sergeant lost his life on duty but the papers upon which he had made application to join the Association had been lost in the post and so his beneficiaries never received any money.

But if a small number of forces were badly organised, most of them were efficiently administered and the Association did make good progress. One very prophetic statement was reported to the Association at its 1869 annual meeting in London. Mr W. G. Turrell, the Head Constable of Cambridge Borough Police, said, "I hope that many of the boroughs which now hold themselves aloof from the Association, will be induced to join. The benefits are far beyond those of an ordinary life assurance company. Only a short time ago, a gentleman connected with a large life assurance company was staying with me and on going through the matter of the Association, said it was bound to improve in time and that it would become a sort of assurance association at a saving of 90% in the working of ordinary societies."

But good news is quickly broadcast and word of the benefits of membership of the PMAA continued to spread. More police officers were joining. By 1870, membership was 5,298; officers of a Dock Police Force and a River Police Force sought permission to become members but were rejected as they were not under the control of either a county or borough chief police officer but the increasing numbers, welcome though they were, also meant extra administrative work. The question of raising a regular sum to cover administrative costs had been aired at the Bath annual meeting and it was decided to levy a rate of one penny from every member to cover expenses – this would produce something around £18. The question of paying expenses to the secretary was also aired. Superintendent Young maintained that he wanted no salary for his secretarial duties even though he was now spending up to four hours a day on Association work, but he did agree to accept travelling expenses for attending meetings.

Even at this stage, the PMAA did not have any office premises, Superintendent Young working from either his home or his police office in Woburn, Bedfordshire. This effected a huge saving on the costs of running and maintaining office accommodation.

By 1871, a separate Widowers' List had been created, with subscriptions of one penny, and the HMI of the Scottish Police Forces became a member.

By now, with the Widowers' List and ordinary members combined, there was a total of 8,864 members out of a national total of police officers of around 35,000. The 'magic' figure of 10,000 ordinary members was already being discussed because it was felt that a membership of more than 10,000 would be too difficult to administer.

Already, the costs were exceeding income. In 1871, the penny rate levied for administrative costs raised £21. 16s. 0d whereas expenditure was more than £28. The balance was met from savings made in earlier years, but it was a situation which would increase as membership rose. And with a rising membership, so the number of deaths would increase; it was currently averaging about thirty each year. In view of the need for control over expenditure, a treasurer was appointed but it was now realised that perhaps some control over membership should be exercised.

For a society of this kind, it is quite extraordinary that there was no requirement for a medical examination nor even a medical certificate as a condition of membership. It was pointed out that some officers were putting off joining until they felt unwell – then they would join as late as possible in the belief that their dependants would benefit for as little outlay as possible. In Scotland, there was no superannuation scheme and so officers were unable to draw pensions. As a consequence, they continued to work until they were literally on the edge of the grave.

The PMAA found itself with lots of aged Scottish members, with all the attendant risks of having members of such advanced years. The Association then conducted a modest survey of deaths and calculated that the average age of death for a serving Association member was 40 years. This was not regarded as abnormally low at that time. The notion of a medical examination was therefore aired but no decision reached.

General Cartwright, HM Inspector General of Constabulary produced a generous show of support by donating £10 each year for the benefit of police widows and when he raised this to £20 in 1872, the Scottish HMI, Colonel Kinloch responded with £10 per year for Scottish widows. When General Cartwright died in 1873, he was succeeded by his son, Major Fairfax Cartwright, a Member of Parliament, who continued to donate generously for the benefit of police widows and in 1874, the Honourable C. Carnegie was appointed HMI for what were described as The Scotch Police Forces. He also continued to give generously for the benefit of Scottish widows.

But problems were ahead.

In 1872 there was an epidemic of smallpox which resulted in 114 deaths of Association members – until now, there had only been 199 in the entire history of the PMAA and this massive increase in just one year presented immense difficulties in collecting subscriptions. Nonetheless, due to the efforts of Superintendent Young, the able secretary, and the authorised officers, the Association was able to cope.

It was a tough time, however, and it did reveal some of the Association's weaknesses. For example, the difference in the rates of subscription and the confusion over ranks and classes of membership continued to cause problems, especially with officers being promoted and unable to decide when or if they should change from one class of contribution to another. It was also suggested that police pensioners be allowed to have their own list, but the problems of collecting their subscriptions would cause yet even more worries to the hard pressed authorised officers. There were the constant worries over the delays in collecting subscriptions and yet in spite of all this, the PMAA was being successful. In 1874, ordinary membership rose to 6,400 and it was now decided to hold the annual meetings in June instead of August with the financial year ending on the last day of February each year.

But around this time, one name was becoming synonymous with the Association. It was that of the Chairman of Committee, Charles Stretten, the Deputy Chief Constable of Cambridgeshire and Huntingdonshire. He was a founder-member of the PMAA, having attended its very first meeting. He assumed the duties of secretary in 1875 upon the death of the loyal and hard-working Superintendent Young and filled the dual role of chairman and secretary until a new secretary, Thomas Hewson, was appointed. But when Hewson died a few months later, Stretten once again took over as secretary; he also took over as president when the president failed to attend meetings.

If one man shouldered the responsibility for the progress of the PMAA at that time, it was Mr Charles Stretten. He had been elected Chairman of Committee in 1872 at the age of 42, which was then around the average age of death for members of the PMAA!

His Chief Constable, Admiral Davies, was President of the

PMAA and sadly, he died shortly afterwards, in 1877. Major Fairfax Cartwright, MP, was elected President and so the PMAA found itself with a voice in Parliament. In fact, it was Cartwright who fought in Parliament for the standardisation of police pensions but his work for the police and for the PMAA was shortlived. He died on 2nd February 1880 at the age of 57 and was succeeded as President of the PMAA by Admiral Christian, RN, the Chief Constable of Gloucestershire.

In the latter years of the century, the PMAA continued in its accepted format – there was still no reserve fund and money was collected for each separate death, there were enormous problems and lengthy delays in the collection of subscriptions and apart from periodic changes in personnel, there was little excitement in its progress although it did continue to attract members.

In 1883, however, there was one important change to the Association's rules. At a meeting held in Birmingham, it was decided to introduce a medical qualification for membership.

Bearing in mind that the average age of death was still in the early 40s, it was decided that anyone over the age of 36 must obtain a medical certificate from a doctor before being admitted to the PMAA. Some felt this was not necessary – one committee member said that authorised officers were perfectly capable of deciding whether or not a man was fit enough to join! In spite of this rule change, one authorised officer did admit a man aged more than 36 – he was, in fact, 47 when he joined but died soon afterwards. His age was then revealed, and it was discovered that the same authorised officer had enrolled another eight members, all over the permitted age. This was accredited to the zeal of the authorised officer because every other member of his force had joined the Association. He'd accomplished his 100% membership drive by enrolling the forbidden nine. But the eight survivors were expelled and their subscriptions were returned.

The Police Service Advertiser and later the *Police Guardian* magazines were both in decline and a new police magazine called *The*

Police Chronicle was making its presence felt. It offered its support to the PMAA while the Association's new President, Colonel Crabbe, the HMI for the Midlands, was involved in a fatal traffic accident. He was being driven along the High Street in Chelmsford by Major Poyntz, the Chief Constable of Essex, when their horse bolted. It killed a woman, injured another and knocked Colonel Crabbe unconscious. He was unable to attend the next annual meeting.

A curious problem arose in 1888 when it was learned that some officers were making wills and bequeathing legacies to persons other than those who had been nominated on their PMAA enrolment forms. If an officer nominated a beneficiary when joining the PMAA, would a subsequent will naming another person alter the situation? These problems might have been due to an oversight or a lapse of memory following the passage of time, but the problem of changed nominees was also creating some worries. Some officers got married, for example, and then failed to change the records of the names of their nominees. Authorised officers were suddenly finding that a wife and family existed for a man who, according to their records, was single and so all authorised officers were asked to ensure that force records were kept up to date. An enormous amount of time was wasted due to inaccurate records. The PMAA decided, however, that it would ignore the instructions of wills – it could only award its monies to those persons nominated by its members in its own records, and if the members wished to change their nominees, then it was the personal responsibility of each so to do.

In 1882, a new member of committee was appointed, a man who was to serve for many years and who was later to be closely associated with the PMAS – he was Superintendent E. Holmes of Leicestershire Constabulary, and in 1887, a new secretary was appointed.

He was to prove a huge success – he was Mr Ellis Crisp, a retired Superintendent from Staffordshire Constabulary. Like all

MR EDWARD HOLMES, OBE

Edward Holmes was the last President of the old Police Mutual Assurance Association when it ended its life in 1921, having been a member of its Committee from 1882 and Chairman since 1892. He also attended the first annual meeting of the Police Mutual Assurance Society and became one of its most ardent supporters. He was a remarkable man. He joined the Leicestershire Constabulary as a clerk and Inspector in 1875, becoming a Superintendent only a year later. He was appointed Deputy Chief Constable in 1885 and became Chief Constable in 1889, a post he was to hold for 39 years. He had been a policeman for 53 years and was still serving at the age of 80. He died in 1928. His work for the PMAS is documented within this book but in addition he was a keen cricketer, and a member of Leicestershire County Cricket Club for many years. He was President in 1899 and was a member of the committee in 1872 when a United South of England Eleven played Leicestershire – and among the players was the legendary W.G. Grace. A prominent Freemason, he succeeded Earl Ferrers as Provincial Grand Master in 1913, but one of his strengths was his astonishing rapport with the miners of the Leicestershire coalfields. So strong was their respect for him that, in a riot situation during the General Strike, he personally spoke to the assembled men whereupon they halted their activities.

secretaries, he would work from home; he lived at Stone in Staffordshire, just one of a long line of Staffordshire officers who have been associated with the PMAA and the PMAS.

A procedural problem arose in 1888 when it was discovered that some chief constables were causing mischief at annual meetings by ordering large numbers of their officers to attend and to vote according to the chief constable's instructions. The precise nature of such mischief was not revealed, but the Committee did decide that only one member of any force should have a vote at the annual meeting, and preferably that should be the authorised officer.

It was in that year that ordinary membership of the PMAA reached 10,000 for the first time and this highlighted the increasing problems of administering a large membership. The Committee now discussed whether or not to restrict membership to no more than 10,000 or to expand, with the resultant rise in the costs of administration. It was decided to defer that decision for one more year, knowing that any increase would result in more work and more collecting of monies by the authorised officers. They worked so hard for no pay and had very few resources. As one member said, "Authorised officers are worthy of a good deal more than is given to them – at least they should be given envelopes!"

Delays in collecting the monies due and handing them over to the beneficiaries continued to be a problem which dogged the PMAA. There is no doubt that the system for collecting subscriptions was laborious and very inefficient. Another problem was created by the rising number of deaths. As more members joined, it was inevitable that the number of deaths increased and some officers openly declared that they would not have become members had they known how much they would have to pay out. Changes to nominees, promotions and late applications all added to the increasing work load of authorised officers.

In 1892, Stretten found himself acting as President yet again, and so his post as chairman at that annual meeting was taken by

Mr E. Holmes of Leicestershire, but only for that one meeting. In the following year, 1893, the Association recorded 147 deaths, just below an average of three per week. Widows were now allowed to join upon the deaths of their husbands, a move which did not increase the number of members, but some widowers were failing to make new nominations upon the deaths of their wives. This caused great problems of administration with long delays in trying to establish the beneficiaries of collected funds; worse still, there were some false claims and so a new form was devised. This was partly due to there being rival claims for the benefits and partly from a need for greater efficiency, but completion of this form had to be witnessed, a move which eliminated many false claims.

There was still the vexed question of whether to restrict membership to 10,000. It hovered about that mark depending upon the number of deaths each year, and the average age of death had now crept up to the mid-fifties. With 10,000 members, a beneficiary of a member of the Half-Crown list received £100, a member of the 6d list (a new list open to inspectors and sergeants) received £60 and those on the penny lists received £48. Constables continued to pay one penny, but members of the Widowers and Widows Lists also paid one penny. As the end of the century approached, there was still no decision about restricting membership. By 1899, there was a total of 10,389 members.

With the new century, there came a new secretary, Mr Joseph Howe – he was to remain for many years and was in fact, the first secretary of the new organisation which was to follow – it would be called the Police Mutual Assurance Society. Like his earlier colleagues, he worked from home for it is perhaps worthy of record that the PMAA still did not have a formal office – its first secretary worked from home and so did all the others. Mr Howe worked from a semi-detached house in Teignmouth. It was No 10 Ferndale Road and this was later to become the first office of the PMAS.

It was in 1900 that there was a change in the conditions of

membership and perhaps this was introduced as a means of reducing or at least controlling numbers.

The age of joining the PMAA without a medical certificate was reduced to 30, although no such restriction was placed on widows. There was also a renewed suggestion that a reserve fund

The first office, a semi-detached house at Teignmouth, Devon

would be wise but no restriction was imposed on the number of members. Membership continued to hover around the 10,000 mark, and the chief problem in the early years of this century was still one of a long delay between a member's death and the payment of monies due. It seemed impossible to reduce this although the time had fallen to an average of about 44 days. It was pointed out, however, that out of every £1 collected, 19s. 10d (99p) went to the beneficiaries. In other words, for every 240 pennies collected, 238 went to the beneficiaries, with just two going towards administrative costs. The expenses of the Society were remarkably low. In the year 1st March 1901 to 28th February 1902, for example, the expenses were only £249. Out of this, £120 was for the secretary's salary (the job was now a salaried post and not undertaken by a serving police officer, although he was elected annually). Most of the income was from the one penny rate which was still being levied, although an increase in costs now led to a 2d levy being imposed that year. A modest £3. 11s. 4d was received from the sale of rule books, this being seen as a minor means of raising funds.

In 1903, one committee member, Mr Leonard Dunning, the Chief Constable of Liverpool, decided that a tough line should be taken with late payers.

He had been an authorised officer and did accept there were problems in collecting pennies from pensioners, but could not excuse serving officers. He said that all late payers should be struck off the register for two months. Even so, delays continued to plague the Association, sometimes involving sums outstanding of up to £2,000. In later years, the Association published a list of its late payers, but there were growing numbers of complaints from members about the variation in the amounts of cash received. That depended, of course, upon the number of members at any given time and this did tend to fluctuate.

In 1904, the Chief Constable of Glamorgan caused upset by forming The Glamorgan County Constabulary Mutual Benefit

Association and then compelling every member of his force to join. There was no option – Rule 1 said that all 367 members must join and they decided that they could not afford to be members of both Associations, and so the PMAA found its membership reduced by 367, although Glamorgan's pensioners continued with their membership.

There was some unhappiness about having pensioners as members and some voices began to suggest a limit for their membership, say five years after retirement, or perhaps ten? Should they be asked to pay subscriptions in advance? And what about ex-police officers, who had either been dismissed or who had left to pursue other careers? Should they be allowed to benefit?

Added to all this was the vexed question of the never-ending delays in paying out the monies due, even though this was now being done by the treasurer. Chief constables no longer paid monies to dependants; when the cash was collected, it was sent to the treasurer who was responsible for paying the recipient. But the delays were onerous and saddening.

The 1908 annual meeting at the Shire Hall in Haverfordwest was noteworthy for two reasons. First was the absence of the President, Mr Charles Stretten. His post was taken at that meeting by Mr E. Holmes who was chairman and in apologising for that absence, Mr Holmes said "Mr Stretten is not as young as he was." In fact, he was 78 years old and still serving as a chief police officer.

The second item of importance was that an entirely new system of operation was proposed. It was suggested that the old system of differing contributions be abandoned and that a fixed payment be instituted.

It was also added that the advice of an actuary had been sought but that his report had only just been received.

It was too late and too lengthy for discussion at that meeting, but copies would be printed and circulated to committee members for their consideration. By the time they had digested this, the committee found themselves considering radical changes to the PMAA. The actuary proposed that there were:

(a) fixed contributions

(b) fixed payments

(c) a reserve fund

With a reserve fund of, say, £10,000, cheques for the benefit of nominees could be paid immediately, but these changes terrified many police officers. They were deeply suspicious of change and lots of them totally misunderstood the motives of the members of the PMAA committee. Some thought they were wanting to pay themselves salaries, some thought the committee members were wanting to line their own pockets, some thought the PMAA was in dire financial straits, some suspected that funds had been misappropriated and others wrote vitriolic letters to police periodicals to denounce the changes. For many, the sum of £10,000 was a mythical figure and beyond their belief – how could their modest Society save such a huge amount and why? Why keep it instead of paying it to beneficiaries who were in need? It was to take a long time and a lot of persuasion by the Association before the changes were implemented.

But the changes were implemented, if only gradually. By 1911, the consulting actuary, Mr Hudson, supported by an eminent London actuary, produced a plan for fixed payments.

He proposed that, in the future, the one penny list members paid 4½d per week to produce £45 at death; the 6d list members paid 10d per week to produce £95 at death; the Half-Crown (2s. 6d) list members paid 1s. 4d. per week to produce £110 at death, and those on the Widows and Widowers List paid 2½d per week to produce £30 at death.

As soon as death was authenticated, the secretary would authorise payment and a cheque would be issued; the above payments would allow for a small excess to be paid into the Reserve Fund. The Reserve Fund would be managed by three trustees and the Association's books would be audited. To begin the new scheme, a small amount of working capital was needed and it was proposed that all members pay two shillings a year for five years; this would produce £2,500, and the Lloyds Banking Company would be asked to invest some of the capital. It seems that most officers could accept these proposals and so, on lst October 1911, they were incorporated in the rules of the Association. There were still different scales of subscription for differing ranks and already questions were being asked about this – why couldn't everyone pay the same?

It was an important and far-reaching change and when the next annual meeting occurred in June 1912 the Association could report that it now held the useful sum of £450 in its Reserve Fund. That was after only five months, i.e. October 1911 until the end of February 1912.

It was at the 1912 meeting that PC Cox of Derby then put another idea to the committee – he suggested that the PMAA be registered under the Friendly Societies Act, a move which would bring further benefits. The senior officers ummed and aahed but agreed it was a good idea and that his proposal would be studied, and PC Cox followed with a suggestion that, because all ranks were represented by the Association, there should be a constable on the Committee of Management. The committee thought about that too, and said that if one was elected, he (or perhaps a sergeant) should come from Birmingham due to the ease of travelling to committee meetings.

By 1913, the new schemes were working well and the PMAA could report some interest on its deposits – £4. 12s. 0d to be precise, and the reserve fund had risen to £2,933 14s. 7d. It was decided that the new schemes would continue for three years to see if they were viable.

But by the time of the annual meeting in June 1915 there was a whole new set of worries to be dealt with. War had broken out in 1914 and so members of the committee, due to meet in Edinburgh, were filled with a sense of foreboding. Many police officers had been called to join the army and the navy and the possibility of many deaths could not be ignored. Some were talking of 1,000 deaths of police officers. But first, the venue of the annual meeting was changed so that it would be more central for the committee members in what were described 'uncertain times'.

It was therefore held on 15th June 1914, in the Assembly Rooms at Leicester. Mr Charles Stretten, MVO, could not attend but was elected President yet again, now being known as The Father of the Association.

The chairman was Mr E. Holmes, Chief Constable of Leicestershire whose record of attendance was impressive – on one occasion, the date of Leicester Quarter Sessions was changed so that he could attend the PMAA meeting, and on another occasion he travelled from America to attend. He had not missed a committee meeting in 23 years. In an otherwise gloomy meeting, there was a moment of happiness when, in recognition of his services to the Association, Mr Holmes was presented with a sideboard, a solid silver tea tray, cake basket, two sauce bowls, teapot, tantalus (a decanter container), cabinet of silver cutlery and serviette rings. There was also a cheque for 100 guineas (£105), the money coming from all members of the Association.

On a more sombre note, the question of police officers serving in HM Forces was discussed. Clearly, they were at great risk and the committee was faced with the possibility of having to impose special levies to cater for the risks involved. Even by the time of that meeting, the death rate of Association members had risen dramatically – 34 already from the war alone – but after a lengthy discussion, it was agreed that no changes to subscriptions would be made. The fixed rates would continue as earlier agreed.

By 1916, Mr Stretten had retired as Chief Constable of his force, aged 86 but he was still President of the PMAA. In that year, a further 59 police officers were killed on active service with HM Forces and the numbers of Association members fell, partly due to some policemen failing to subscribe their pennies while on active service. But for the Association it was bad news. The additional work led to a deficiency of £400 in the ordinary expenses and by 1917, there was even worse news. Due to police officers being called up for HM Services, there was a further reduction in PMAA membership and this was aggravated by a lack of recruiting. There had been no new recruits to the police service for 2½ to 3 years, recruits having always been a rich source of new PMAA members. Expenses had also increased and although the Association had begun the year with a balance of £1,400 in its reserve fund, that had now dwindled to a mere £212. Without the war, the reserve fund would have been in the region of £6,000–£7,000.

The PMAA was now faced with an immense problem. The war was continuing and it was inevitable that there would be more deaths but there would be no further recruits to help bolster income. The Association had three choices – (a) to realise a part or the whole of the Association's modest investments; (b) to reduce the amounts paid to nominees, or (c) to increase subscriptions. In the latter case, an increase of the basic amount from one penny to two pence would produce £2,097.

It was with great reluctance that the Committee had no alternative but to increase subscriptions. It decided to raise them by one penny but only for a maximum of 30 weeks. By doing so, the committee increased the balance from £212 to a useful £1,080 but the troubles were not over. A terrible epidemic of influenza broke out just after the war and so the PMAA found itself having to pay out yet more monies for a further 54 influenza victims in addition to 73 from the final year of the war. 276 police officers had been killed on war service and the net result for the PMAA was that, by the year ending February 1919 it had a deficit of £336. 16s. 5½d. Its reserve fund was exhausted, but it still had some £2,000 invested and this was bringing in a modest amount of interest. For the future security of the Association there was talk

35

of deducting 5% from the sums due to nominees as a means of covering expenses. In all respects, it was a fraught and very worrying period.

There was a slight glimmer of hope of recovery because police recruiting resumed after the war and 200 new members had joined the Association. Even so, it was decided, with reluctance, to continue the extra levy of one penny for a further short time.

When the PMAA met at Llandudno in June 1920, there was further bad news. Its long-serving President, Charles Stretten, had died on 23rd August 1919, at the age of 89.

He had joined Cambridgeshire Police on 4th December 1851, aged 21, and had joined the PMAA on 1st March 1867. He was a member of its first meeting at Windsor in August 1866, was elected Chairman in 1873, Vice President in 1892 and President in 1898, a total of 52 years service with the Association.

The new President was to be Mr Edward Holmes who had been a member of committee since 1882 and Chairman since 1892, thus achieving some 28 years service. Among the officers who attended this meeting were an inspector from Birmingham City Police; he was Inspector B.D. Pinkerton, known as Ben; the Chief Constable of Northampton, Mr F. H. Mardlin, Major H. P. Hunter, the Assistant Chief Constable of Staffordshire and Mr Roderick Ross, MVO, CBE, the Chief Constable of Edinburgh, all of whom were to play an important role in forming the new PMAS.

One wonders what would have been the impressions of dear old Mr Stretten if he could have been at that 1920 meeting, because it was reported that, in spite of all the trauma of the war years, the PMAA had survived. There was comfort or even joy in the news that 881 new members had joined, and then, after all its payments and expenditure had been settled, it still had a balance of £708. It had not been necessary, after all, to make the 5% deduction from the monies due to nominees. And during its life, the PMAA had paid out more than half a million pounds in

MR F.H. MARDLIN

F.H. Mardlin, the Chief Constable of Northampton, was the first Chairman of the Police Mutual Assurance Society. He had always taken a keen interest in the welfare of his men and was an active worker for the old Police Mutual Assurance Association, becoming its Chairman a few months before it ceased to exist. He continued as Chairman of the PMAS when it was formed in 1921, but retired at the first Annual General Meeting in 1922 due to ill-health. There is no doubt that the part he played, as Chairman of both organisations, in conducting the negotiations which led to the merger of the PMAA and the PMAS, indicated superb qualities of leadership and compassion.

The son of a police officer, Mr Mardlin joined Bedfordshire Constabulary in 1875, then transferred to Newcastle-upon-Tyne Detective Force in 1878 where he became a First Class Sergeant. He then joined Leicester City Police in 1881 as a Detective Inspector where he dealt successfully with a range of serious crimes, following which he was appointed Chief Constable of Northampton in 1887. He was then the youngest Chief Constable in England.

In addition to providing very modern welfare facilities for his men, he founded the Northampton Good Samaritan Society in 1893, a scheme later adopted in many other areas of Britain. He retired on 31st December 1923, having completed 51 years' service.

benefits. The Chairman said it was a report of which all could be proud.

But it was clear that major alterations were necessary if the concept of a police mutual assurance society was to survive, and the members of the committee were asked to consider radical changes. An approach for State aid had been made to the Home Secretary under the existing provisions of the Police Act of 1919, but he replied that he could not assist unless the PMAA became soundly based on an actuarial basis. As the PMAA did not have that necessary basis, it lost no time in re-arranging its affairs so that it could comply with those conditions. Coincidentally, a letter was received from the recently formed Police Federation asking for quotations for an insurance scheme for members of the Federation. The PMAA replied that it was interested and suggested a meeting which would produce an acceptable scheme of insurance and so, bearing in mind these two new possible developments, the PMAA Committee appointed a sub-committee.

Its purpose was to liaise with a highly respected actuary called Mr J. Murray Laing, FIA, FFA, an actuary with the Britannic Assurance Company in Birmingham, and to produce a scheme which was acceptable to both the Police Federation and the Home Office. That sub-committee comprised Messrs Holmes, Mardlin, Hunter, Pinkerton, Myers and Joseph Howe, the secretary. In time, Mr Murray Laing produced two life assurance schemes – one was a Whole Life Scheme covering members aged 18 to 70 years, and the second was an Endowment Assurance Scheme.

The first would accommodate all the existing members of the PMAA and the second was a totally new idea. In his opinion, both schemes were actuarially sound.

The sub-committee met the Police Federation in London on 21st January 1921 to present their ideas and they were accompanied by Mr Murray Laing. The outcome was that if the Home Secretary agreed that the proposals were actuarially sound, then the Police Federation would commend the schemes to its members.

In a letter dated 18th June 1921, the Home Secretary, having consulted with the Government Actuary, did express an opinion that both schemes were actuarially sound and added that if the local authorities involved in the scheme found it acceptable, then the Government would agree to pay its grant of 50% of the local authority costs. The Home Secretary also suggested that the new Society be registered as a Friendly Society and that its management expenses should not exceed 5% of income.

There were some other conditions which could be easily complied with, although one condition was that the new Society must attract sufficient members to secure the basis for working out the averages contained in the Actuary's calculations. In the minutes of that historic meeting is the following paragraph: *It was decided that the adoption of the schemes be taken together and on being put to the meeting, those suggested by the committee were carried unanimously.*

Mr Pinkerton then invited the PMAA to hold its next annual meeting in Birmingham, and this was accepted. It was held in the Victoria Law Courts in Birmingham on 21st June 1921, and it was destined to be the final meeting of the Police Mutual Assurance Association. The President, Mr Hunter of Leicester, gravely announced that there was important business to transact.

Their task today was to reconstruct the old PMAA to form a new society. He accepted there would be differences of opinion but said that if the new society commended itself to the police forces of Britain, then members of the old one would continue their membership within the new. The old PMAA would continue in name until the new society had been established and he introduced Mr Murray Laing who had drawn up some tables to illustrate the proposed new benefits.

The assembled committee members and other delegates heard the final annual report of the PMAA and one can speculate that there was much sadness at its impending end. That decision ended the Police Mutual Assurance Association and gave birth to the Police Mutual Assurance Society.

The last President of the PMAA was Mr E. Holmes, Chief Constable of Leicestershire but the first President of the new PMAS was to be an HMI, Sir Leonard Dunning, Bart, a former authorised officer and ex-Chief Constable of Liverpool.

The last secretary of the PMAA was Mr Joseph Howe and he became the first secretary of the PMAS; the last Chairman of the Committee of Management of the PMAA was Mr F. H. Mardlin, the Chief Constable of Northampton and he became the first Chairman of the Committee of Management of the PMAS. He chaired a meeting in Birmingham on Thursday 14th September 1922 which formally closed the accounts of the Police Mutual Assurance Association.

But in the trauma of those final days, no one mentioned the man who started it all. The identity of 'Verdad' remained a secret as the young PMAS somewhat nervously began what was to become a long and highly successful life.

CHAPTER 2

EARLY DAYS

1922 – 1949

The mystery surrounding the identity of 'Verdad' might have intrigued followers of the adventures of Sherlock Holmes. They might well have believed that the great fictional detective was interested in 'Verdad' as the anonymous originator of the PMAS because a report of the first Annual Meeting of the new Police Mutual Assurance Society in Bristol (1922) lists two Sherlockian names – Holmes and Moriarty.

But these men were not investigating 'Verdad'; they were two very real senior police officers. The fictitious Holmes and Moriarty had crashed to their deaths over the Reichenbach Falls in Switzerland in 1893. Demands from readers caused their creator, Sir Arthur Conan Doyle, to resurrect the famous duo.

The real Holmes and Moriarty, however, had joined the Committee of Management of the PMAS. Holmes was Mr E. Holmes, the Chief Constable of Leicestershire, and Mr C.C.H. Moriarty was the then Assistant Chief Constable of Birmingham City Police. In the busy world of the modern British police service, those names live on – the name HOLMES is somewhat tenuous in that context but it is the name now applied to a major incident computer known as the Home Office Large Major Enquiry System, thus ensuring that HOLMES continues to solve important crimes.

Mr Holmes, however, had been associated with the old PMAA since 1882, rising to become Chairman of its Committee. There is more detail of his extensive work in Chapter 1. Moriarty is another famous police name, for it is the title given to the police officer's bible – this is a book whose real title is *Police Law*. It was originally written by that same C.C.H. Moriarty. This popular and

MR C.C.H. MORIARTY,
CBE, BA, LLD

The name of Moriarty is one of the best known within British police circles. Not only was Mr C.C.H. Moriarty an outstanding man, he was also a brilliant academic, a highly competent police officer and a Rugby International.

He was born in 1877, the son of an Irish rector and was educated at Trinity College, Dublin. There he gained an honours degree (a BA) and was awarded the first senior Moderatorship and large gold medal, later taking an LLB with honours. Afterwards, his skill at compiling books on criminal law and police procedure earned him a degree of Doctor of Law.

His police career began as a cadet in the Royal Irish Constabulary and he became a District Inspector in 1902, a post he held until 1918. He was then appointed Assistant Chief Constable of Birmingham City Police in 1918, being awarded the OBE in 1925, the King's Police Medal in 1929, a Commander of the Order of St John of Jerusalem in 1936 and the CBE in 1938.

In addition to being a skilled hockey player, he was an outstanding Rugby footballer and in 1899 played forward for Ireland against Wales when Ireland won the Triple Crown.

He became Chief Constable of Birmingham in 1935 and retired in 1941. In his retirement, he relaxed by fishing and gardening but continued to write his range of books on police law and procedure; the best known is his 'Police Law', known throughout the service simply as Moriarty.

Mr Moriarty attended the very first meeting of the PMAS in 1922 and was appointed to its Committee of Management, later becoming one of the Society's Trustees and then a Vice President in

1943. His interest in and support for the PMAS continued until his death in 1958 aged 81.

indispensable volume has been regularly re-published since the first edition in 1929 and it is one of that select range of books known by its author's name rather than its formal title.

This anecdote is just one way of illustrating the manner in which the foundation and development of the Police Mutual Assurance Society has in many ways both echoed and complemented the history of the British police service while attracting the voluntary help of some of its best known personalities.

There is little doubt that the progress of the PMAS owes much to the changes which affected the service, particularly those which occurred around the time of the foundation of the PMAS. It is perhaps wise to digress slightly in order to record those important developments.

For example, the Government and the nation's many police authorities had been made acutely aware of the demands placed upon all police officers; they recognised the risks they endured in the course of their duties, and they appreciated their status within our society.

This awareness was due to publication in 1919 of the first part of the famous Desborough Report. Under the chairmanship of Lord Desborough, the Home Secretary had appointed a committee to consider, *inter alia,* changes in the conditions of service of police officers, and of their rates of pay, allowances and pensions. It was a far reaching and very welcome report and it revolutionised the police service at that time – for example, paragraph 28 of the first part said,

"In view of the evidence which we have heard as to the work of the police and the high standard of qualifications required, we are satisfied that a policeman has responsibilities and obligations which are peculiar to his calling and distinguish him from other public servants and municipal employees, and we consider the police entitled thereby to special consideration in regard to their rate of pay and pensions."

One effect of this was the passing of the Police Act 1919 which had standardised the conditions of service for police officers throughout Great Britain but it had also highlighted the need for strong welfare representation for police officers.

Following the emphasis upon welfare, and with the sanction of the Police Act of 1919, came the formation of the Police Federation whose early letter to the PMAA prompted a change of attitude which in turn led, *inter alia*, to the creation of the PMAS.

The Police Federation had come into existence in 1919 to look after the welfare of all police officers from the rank of constable up to chief inspector, but it had no funds and no reserves which could be utilised for insurance. Furthermore, it then had very little influence. Thus any new society or association would have to raise its own money to pay financial benefits to police officers and their dependants in the event of death. Such a society would also have to encourage its members to save and to plan their financial futures. Police salaries were not very high and so the income would not be great, but many officers had great faith in the idea of a mutual assurance society to cater especially for police officers. After the problems of the PMAA, they were also wise enough to realise that they needed the very best of professional advice – the old PMAA had been run by police officers for police officers, but it lacked a professional knowledge of the insurance world, especially so far as risks and investments were concerned. Any new society would need an actuary who would calculate the financial risks and benefits involved, and who could advise them on investments and all aspects of monetary awareness such as savings and insurance.

Chapter 1 shows how the Committee of the PMAA, along with the Police Federation and with positive help from the Home Secretary, had initiated action which would raise the new Society to a highly professional level.

They had been most fortunate in gaining the marvellous support and wisdom of the actuary, Mr J. Murray Laing. During those preparatory months, he had devised a new scheme with premiums that were actuarially lower than necessary but added

MR JAMES MURRAY LAING
FIA, FFA

It was the actuarial skills of James Murray Laing which established the infant PMAS on such a firm financial foundation and he remained to guide the Society, as its Consulting Actuary, until his death in 1952.

James Murray Laing was born in Glasgow in November 1879, and his first post was as office boy in the Glasgow branch of the old British Empire Mutual Life Office. In March 1903 he joined the London office of the National Mutual Life Association of Australia and in 1905 took top place in the final examination of the Faculty of Actuaries. He became a Fellow of the Institute of Actuaries (Edinburgh) in 1907.

In May 1908 he joined the Britannic Assurance Company where he served for more than 44 years. It was during this service that he became Consulting Actuary to the PMAS, and in spite of his heavy commitments, became Deputy Chairman and Managing Director of the Britannic. He became Vice Chairman of the National Amalgamated Approved Society, Chairman of the Industrial Life Offices Association from 1945 to 1947, senior Vice President of the Institute of Actuaries and President of Birmingham Insurance Institute.

When away from his office, he was an enthusiastic worker for local hospitals and Moseley Presbyterian Church; he was a brilliant speaker, a devoted family man and a person of the highest ideals. The PMAS was indeed fortunate to secure his services and his devotion to its own specialised cause.

that, to make the plan viable, a lump sum was required as a reserve. In other words, he needed a substantial injection of cash which would form that reserve and which could also be invested. He had appealed for help to every police authority which had members affected by the financial problems of the PMAA, and was delighted with their response.

Between them, they had donated £3,687, a considerable sum at that time. With this cash reserve, Mr Murray Laing was able to propose a soundly-based Whole Life Scheme but it was dependent upon a fixed weekly instalment of premiums from all its members. With this secure form of income, his calculations showed that, at the end of a specified period, or in the event of previous death, a guaranteed payment could be made to the beneficiaries.

Murray Laing was then faced with the challenge of convincing police officers that this was a sound investment and he started at the top – his first action was to persuade no less a person than the Home Secretary. It was during that powerful mood of support for the police that the Home Secretary found himself considering the proposed foundation of a brand new specialised insurance scheme for police officers.

Before it could be officially established, it had to have the approval of the Home Secretary as specified in section 9 of the Police Act of 1919. In the aftermath of the failure of the old PMAA, however, the question continued to be asked as to whether the proposed new Society would be able to meet its commitments in the event of a sudden demand upon its rather limited reserve. In those early months, those worries must have remained with the committee members and there can be no doubt that many officers throughout the country were somewhat suspicious of the viability of the new Society.

So could sufficient police officers be persuaded to become members and so make the scheme viable? At least 5,000 members were necessary to make it work. These questions had been considered by the Home Secretary as he studied the application. One very important show of confidence had been provided by Lloyds Bank which had been the banker of the PMAA.

Lloyds confirmed that it would grant overdraft facilities to the new Society so that it could meet all claims which might arise until the Society was able to achieve a credit balance. That decision must surely rank among the wisest investments ever made by a British bank, for Lloyds' role as banker for the PMAA and the PMAS spans more than 80 years. But that decision by the bank had been a major factor in convincing Home Office officials and the Home Secretary of the viability of the proposed PMAS.

The proposal which had been presented to the Home Secretary must have seemed both innovative and perhaps a little risky at that time, but his valued support has been a powerful factor in the continuing success of the PMAS. It has always maintained close links with the Home Office, even to the extent of having some of its annual meetings in Whitehall.

That official approval meant that the new Society, formally renamed the Police Mutual Assurance Society, could begin its work with official backing. That fact alone impressed potential members and another matter which raised the confidence of police officers was that, in September 1921, the PMAS had been registered as a Friendly Society.

Another important factor was that the proposed new Society should be controlled *by* police officers exclusively *for* police officers, albeit with professional assistance. Yet another feature was the appointment of unpaid 'agents' within the police forces of Britain, men who would recruit members of the society and promote its benefits among their fellow officers. These would not be known as agents, however, but would be termed 'Authorised Officers'. The Authorised Officers, a term first used many years earlier by the PMAA, would be police officers who would undertake work for the Society in their spare time for no pay, commission or expenses; they would truly be working for the mutual benefit of themselves and their colleagues, and it would be their task to recruit sufficient members to make the society viable.

The new Society's registration as a Friendly Society would ensure higher benefits for its members because it would pay no income tax on the interest which accrued from its investments, and any dividends would likewise be paid gross. And, furthermore, it was specified in the rules right from the outset that the Society's business must be transacted on an expense ratio not exceeding five per cent of its income from premiums. This low-cost administration made the PMAS the envy of many other insurance companies and it helped it to fulfil the promise that PMAS members get "The most for the least."

It was upon these ideals, and with this foundation, that the new Society began to operate. From the very beginning, it was fortunate in attracting the support and interest of senior and

A view of 161 Corporation Street, Birmingham where the Society rented four rooms

influential police officers. Many leading personalities, with foresight and dedication over the years, have helped to provide the PMAS with its firm foundation. A list of their names, whether acting as members of various committees based at Head Office or as Authorised Officers within police forces, makes fascinating reading. Both Holmes and Moriarty, for example, became Trustees of the PMAS.

Over the years, a host of outstanding officers who have been associated with major developments and innovations within the police service itself have also enjoyed a parallel participation in the development of the PMAS.

This dedication has elevated the Society to its rightful position as a very essential element of the British police service. There is little doubt that Holmes, Moriarty and all those associated with the old PMAA and the PMAS, would be pleased and proud of the current professionalism of the service just as they would be proud of the sound and thriving Society.

But for all their support, both Holmes and Moriarty missed the second annual meeting in Manchester on 18th May 1923. That meeting was to publish the accounts and to discuss the progress of the first full year of activity of the society which had been created from the remnants of the PMAA.

In the months since its foundation, the Committee of Management had worked hard to publicise the benefits of the PMAS and many thousands of leaflets and other literature had been distributed throughout Britain. The result was a very satisfactory influx of members, 1,500 in the last twelve months. However, the tone of that meeting was not entirely congratulatory because there was a deficiency of £530 19s. 11d. in the Management Fund.

This had arisen due to the fact that 5% of members' contributions (as specified in the rules) had been insufficient to defray the expenses incurred during that first year of the Society's existence. Bearing in mind the reason for the decline of the PMAA (Chapter 1), the Management Fund Committee might have been forgiven if they had reacted with dismay to this news, but they did not.

They remained calm and determined, and it is recorded that *"The committee was confident that with the growth of the premium income, and as a result of the energetic steps taken to control future expenditure, the adverse balance would be liquidated before the next actuarial valuation."* By the following year, that figure had been reduced to £407 9s. 10½d, further reducing in the following year to £309 15s. 5½d and finally being cleared by 31st December 1925 in time for the 1926 Annual Meeting. From that time, the infant Society continued to flourish and the deep faith of those early administrators was justified.

The PMAS was on course to become Britain's largest private membership insurance company.

As it grew, the Society emphasised the fact that it encouraged consultation by men from different police forces as they sought to plan benefits for men in every force. The death of a comrade, for example, extended beyond the boundaries of any single police district – and there were many districts at that time. The strength of the PMAS was that it was a self-help organisation – police officers were doing something for themselves without external assistance, and that help came from every rank, from the highest to the lowest, and it was all on a voluntary basis.

Not forgotten, of course, were members of the now defunct Police Mutual Assurance Association; it was their dilemma which had provided the impetus for the new Society. They were given facilities to transfer to the new Society on very favourable terms and the Whole Life Scheme devised by the PMAS was restricted to them. They were given time to apply for the necessary transfer and that facility had ended on 31st March 1922. Thus the Whole Life Scheme membership comprised only members of the old PMAA. The new Endowment Scheme was designed especially for members of the new Society. It was open to serving police officers under the age of 50 and their wives and so, with two branches, the

PMAS began its work. Officially, it had begun operations on 16th January 1922 and its immediate task had been to make itself, and its benefits, known to every police officer in Great Britain.

But sustained work of this kind needs the services of paid administrators as well as premises, stationery and office equipment; during those very early stages, the PMAS had nothing, apart from the remnants of the PMAA plus an enormous reserve of goodwill and a tremendous faith in its own future. While police officers were willing and able to serve on committees and as Authorised Officers, who would do the unavoidable and highly important clerical work?

Among the astonishing fortunes of the PMAS is that the right person seems to arrive on the scene at precisely the right time. The secretary, Joseph Howe, who had steered the PMAA through some of its most difficult times and who had worked on the creation of the PMAS from its first office in a semi-detached house in Teignmouth, Devon, now retired from ill-health. The PMAS sought the appointment of a new secretary. After due deliberation, one of the candidates was appointed.

He was Captain S.A. Wood. A confirmed bachelor who was described as hard-working, indefatigable, conscientious and meticulous in everything he did, he was selected from a list of one hundred and thirty applicants. Captain Wood, as he was always known, held the post for the following thirty-two years until he retired in 1954. In his first months, he had virtually nothing in the way of office furnishings and equipment, and the existing records of the defunct PMAA were less than useful.

Wood's work was of such quality that, after only his first year in office, he was given a huge pay increase — the 1923 Annual Meeting voted to increase his salary from £300 a year to £350 with effect from 1st January 1923. A rise of about £1 a week was very substantial at that time. When Captain Wood retired in 1954, however, the assets of the Society had exceeded £2 million and the Society operated from office premises in Birmingham.

CAPTAIN
S.A. WOOD

The work of Captain Wood in establishing the early PMAS is well documented within these pages. His meticulous work did so much to provide the infant Society with such a firm foundation.

He came from a family which was well known in legal circles in the Midlands, his grandfather, two uncles and brother all being solicitors. Captain Wood, as he was always known to the PMAS, was educated at Bishop Vesey's Grammar School, Sutton Coldfield. During the First World War he was a captain and paymaster of the Cheshire Regiment in Shrewsbury and spent several years of service in the East.

In 1922, he was selected from 130 applicants for the post of Secretary to the PMAS and arrived when the Society had no funds and when its office records were in a state of chaos. When he retired in 1954 at the age of 65, it was a thriving, efficient organisation with assets in excess of £2 million. Upon his retirement, Sir Herbert Hunter paid tribute to his capacity for hard work and his genius in restoring order out of chaos.

Captain Wood was a keen golfer; he was a member and former captain of Sutton Coldfield Golf Club and at the time of his death was one of six Vice Presidents of the club. He was a dedicated churchman and keen gardener who loved music and literature. In addition, he was known as a good speaker at the many functions he attended.

It was remarkable progress – he had certainly responded to the faith placed in him and he had most certainly earned his salary!

There is little doubt that the beginning of the PMAS was somewhat infirm but it was soon very clear that proper office accommodation was needed. With a staff of one male clerk and two typists, Captain Wood set about establishing his permanent operating base. It was decided that Birmingham was the most convenient location from which to administer the new Society for it is very close to the centre of Great Britain and had good means of communication by rail and road. The rooms he sought had to be capable of accommodating what had then grown from one man into one man with a small staff and some office equipment. In 1923, therefore, the first Head Office was established in what has been described as 'a four roomed garret'. Others described it as 'that damned garret' or 'shabby, down-at-heel and most unattractive'. But it was home to the infant Society, and it was in Pitman Buildings, 161 Corporation Street in Birmingham, premises rented from the City of Birmingham Estates Department. There were four rooms. Captain Wood used one, another contained wooden filing cabinets and was used by the typist; the clerical staff used the third and the fourth was a stock room. Working conditions were undoubtedly Dickensian but as a consequence, the Society re-established its earlier links with those officers of the Midlands whose efforts had led to its creation.

This centre of PMAS operations has remained in the Midlands ever since and in establishing its first Head Office in Birmingham it also consolidated its association with members of the local police forces, Birmingham City and Staffordshire in particular. Officers from those forces had played such an important role in the development of the PMAA and in the early years of the PMAS; indeed, they continue to be represented in its continuing development.

Other important events also took place in those formative months. One was the appointment of Sir Leonard Dunning as the first President of the Police Mutual Assurance Society. A former Authorised Officer and ex-Chief Constable of Liverpool, he had been on the committee of the PMAA but was now an Inspector of Constabulary. He was to serve as PMAS President from 1922 until 1937.

Sir Leonard was a modest man and very popular. There is no doubt that his association with the new Society convinced many doubters of its merits. When he was re-elected to the office of President at the 1923 Annual Meeting upon completion of his first year, he suggested that it might be wiser to appoint someone with a practical, working interest in the Society. He even said he had done little except attend meetings – but the membership disagreed. They knew he had in fact worked very hard, often behind the scenes, and had used his influence and his past experience with the PMAA to help establish the PMAS in those early, somewhat fraught times.

As one committee member said, "The Presidency could not be in better hands." Throughout his long service as President, he continued to be the most modest of men, always stressing that he would willingly stand down if the membership wished to elect anyone else. He said he would not be slighted by an alternative choice – but the membership always felt he was the ideal man. He was once described as being 'a great inspiration' to the Society and his appointment began the tradition that an incumbent Inspector of Constabulary be President of the Society. Later, in 1963 when the office of Chief Inspector of Constabulary was created, it became customary to appoint Chief HMIs as President of the PMAS.

The office of Chairman of Committee had also to be filled and this revealed a most striking personality. He was the then Inspector B.D. Pinkerton of Birmingham City Police who was later described as 'redoubtable' and a cornerstone of the Society. He had witnessed the end of the PMAA and was described as a man with immense charisma, wisdom and drive all enhanced by his formidable physical appearance. It is fair to say that Pinkerton's inspired and imaginative drive helped to formulate the secure basis upon which the society has flourished ever since. He rose through the ranks to become Superintendent within his own force, and was the Society's Chairman of Committee for more than thirty years, retiring in 1952. It was a tremendous record.

Bearing in mind that the PMAS has always recognised a man for his ability to further the aims of the Society rather than the stature of his police rank, it is interesting to look at the composition of the General Committee in 1923 – it comprised (in order of votes cast by the membership): Superintendent F.W. Myers of Leicestershire, Inspector B.D. Pinkerton of Birmingham, Chief Constable T. Davies of Portsmouth, Police Constable T. Simpkins of Luton, Chief Inspector W. Southwell of Salford, Assistant Chief Constable C.C. Staunton of East Suffolk and Sergeant J.R. Stansfield of Salford. It would be difficult to find a broader range of ranks on such a small committee of police officers.

But this is another of the strengths of the PMAS. From the very beginning, it was recognised that officers from the lower ranks were just as important in the Society's management as those carrying higher rank. It has always been a feature of the PMAS that the constitution of its management is based upon the broadest possible foundations.

It was emphasised at the 1925 Annual Meeting, for example, that there was nothing to prevent any member of the Society, even if he was the youngest constable, from securing a place on the General Committee, provided, of course, that he had proved his value. It was also stressed that membership of the General Committee was by ballot which enhanced its democratic status.

Extract from the 1931 PMAS diary

THE
Police Mutual Assurance Society's
POCKET
Almanac and Diary
1931

CONTAINING INFORMATION
USEFUL TO ALL
POLICE OFFICERS.

SUPERINTENDENT
B.D. PINKERTON, KPM

Ben Pinkerton helped to establish the Society from its very beginnings and then guided it through its difficult early days.

Ben Pinkerton came from police stock, his father being Head Constable in the Royal Irish Constabulary and later a magistrates' clerk. Ben joined Birmingham City Police in March 1900, was promoted sergeant in 1913 and Inspector in March 1919. He was then placed in charge of Digbeth Police School which was established to cope with the large number of recruits following the end of World War I. Thousands passed through his hands and the high reputation of Pinkerton and his training methods became known across the nation. He left the Training School upon promotion to Chief Inspector in 1924, having become renowned as an outstanding instructor. His promotion to Superintendent came in 1928. He was also founder of Birmingham Police Golfing Society, President of the Police Band and was known for his cycling abilities. He was awarded the King's Police Medal in 1936 for distinguished service.

His work for the PMAS is shown within the pages of this book and he was appointed Chairman of the Management Committee in 1922, a post he held until 1952 when he was made an Honorary Vice President in recognition of his work. He died at his home in Ludlow in January 1953, aged 75.

At that time, the number of police forces in Great Britain was far greater than it is today even if some were not listed among those who supported the PMAS. The Royal Ulster Constabulary was not included, but England, Scotland and Wales were then dotted with over 260 forces. Some were tiny Borough Forces with less than twenty officers while the larger County Forces, like Lancashire, exceeded a thousand. The ambition of the PMAS was to have a presence in every one, however small, in the form of an Authorised Officer and by as early as 1923 there were 211 Authorised Officers within 260 police forces. Today, there are some 600 Authorised Officers at Force and Divisional level in the 60 police forces represented by the PMAS – these include the forces of the Ports of London and Liverpool, the Atomic Energy Authority Police, Jersey Police, Ministry of Defence Police, British Transport Police, Isle of Man Police, Guernsey Police and the Royal Ulster Constabulary whose officers were admitted to membership in 1958.

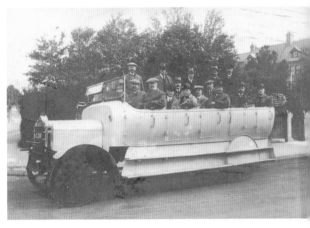

An outing by charabanc. Authorised Officers enjoying the fresh air at Llandudno 1949

In those early days, with such a large number of police forces, it was evident that many of them had created their own benefit societies which were constituted in various ways.

It was also clear that members of such societies believed theirs were superior to all others, or at least adequate for their intended purpose. Mr Murray Laing feared otherwise.

At the 1924 Annual Meeting of the PMAS in Plymouth (a week before a royal visit by HM The Queen of Rumania), he stressed that such societies were all very well *if their members understood their nature.* Unless those societies were actuarially solvent, there was a great danger of them not being able to meet their commitments. He said that an insurance society could be accumulating wealth but at the same time be going headlong into ruin. The old PMAA was one example.

Some smaller societies regarded the PMAS as a threat to their existence, even if some had already disappeared; some officers even felt that the PMAS was working against local charities and it became evident that the PMAS had a lot of work to undertake in convincing officers of its true merit. It was the words of Lieutenant-Colonel H.P. Hunter OBE, the Assistant Chief Constable of Staffordshire, which helped achieve this. In 1924, he said there was no similar society in England or even in the world which could offer such advantageous terms as were given by the Endowment Scheme of the PMAS. The annual report for 1923 showed there was absolute security not only promised but completely attained, and he added that this should cause the PMAS to appeal to all police officers.

Police Mutual Assurance Society.

Investments Exceed		Total Membership
£56,000.	31/12/24	13,448.

OVER FIVE HUNDRED MEMBERS have been enrolled in the Endowment Branch since the 1st of January this year.

Full particulars of the Society's attractive Scheme of Life and Investment Assurance may be obtained from any Authorised Officer; or CAPT. S. A. WOOD, Secretary, Police Mutual Assurance Society, 161, Corporation Street, Birmingham

This confidence was echoed by Mr H.H. Sanders, the Chief Constable of Plymouth (the host force) who said he had, that very day, taken out a policy with the PMAS Endowment Scheme.

He added that, in his previous force, he had paid for 21 years into a Provident Fund but on transferring to Plymouth had not received one penny. Mr Murray Laing did not waste that opportunity to reinforce the strength of the PMAS – he drew attention to the fact that under the Endowment Scheme's cash surrender system, a man in similar circumstances to Mr Sanders who was assured with the PMAS, would receive over £40 as a cash surrender value. It became clear that none of the smaller societies could compete and the benefits of membership of the PMAS began to reach a wider audience.

Part of the Society's publicity endeavours was to launch its

Pocket Almanac and Diary. The first was published in 1925 and launched at the Leeds Annual Meeting; it comprised a diary containing other information of interest and use to police officers. Later editions contained abstracts from the Annual Reports of the relevant years, along with a Gazetteer of police forces itemising their chief constables, their authorised establishment of officers, the number who were members of the PMAS and the name of the Force Authorised Officer. There were details of the Police Council for England and Wales, and for Scotland, as well as details of the Police Federations for England and Wales, and for Scotland.

The mass of information included traffic signals, definitions for police officers, the Judges' Rules, duties under the Diseases of Animals Acts, a digest of the Police Pensions Act, 1921, an account of the King's Police Medal, motor index numbers and international marks, lighting-up times, brief details of licences such as gun licences, game licences, hawkers' and pedlars' licences and so forth, postal and telegraphic information and, of course, a calendar – all preceding the weekly diary with its bank holidays, quarter days and phases of the moon.

For such a compact pocket diary, it contained a surprising wealth of valuable facts and information. The diary was continued, with a reduced print order during the Second World War due to restrictions on the use of paper. For example, 16,000 copies were printed in 1939, 7,500 in 1942 and only 3,000 by 1944. Later, the legal definitions it included were issued separately as the PMAS book of 'Useful Definitions for Police Officers', still valued in its updated form as a ready introduction to the study of basic police law.

Another similar device appeared in 1926 – it was the Society's Atlas Blotter, a combined writing pad and pack of eight maps which was issued in the August of that year. Other means of publicity were to follow, such as the PMAS calendar, and these proved highly popular and were an added means of publicising the Society's merits. They complemented the advertisements which appeared in police periodicals and were an additional means of publicising the PMAS, although some types of advertising, such as the desk calendar, were suspended during the 1939–45 war.

If the Desborough Report served to increase the stature of the service in the early 1920s, albeit only among the Government, police authorities and local authorities, then the General Strike of 1926 added a further air of approval from the public. By refusing to join the General Strike, the police distanced themselves from trouble-makers and political activists and showed themselves to be impartial while performing their tough duties. The TUC was angry at the police action, but the public showed their appreciation by contributing generously to 'The Times' Fund which was established to ease the burden of officers who suffered during those traumatic times.

Another bonus was an anonymous donation of £1,500. A generous police supporter had placed £1,500 at the disposal of the Home Secretary, with the proviso that it be used for some police purpose. The Home Secretary, Sir William Joynson-Hicks, Bart (later Viscount Brentford), passed the money to the PMAS where it gave a useful boost to the Whole Life Reserve Fund. As a matter of record, the 1926 Annual Meeting of the PMAS was held at the Home Office and it was attended by Sir William. He took the opportunity to add his own words of appreciation for the unstinting work of the police during the unrest of 1926. He described the police work as admirable and said their efforts had returned the police service to its old position as a friend of the people.

There is little doubt that this period saw the police service at the height of public popularity which in turn led to an increase in membership of the service. More officers meant more potential members of the PMAS which in turn would lead to better benefits for all those who did join. The Annual Meeting of 1926 heard that new members were needed and that the costs of management of the PMAS were still below the 5% specified in the rules – in fact, the cost was less than $4\frac{1}{2}\%$ of the Society's income

The 1926 Annual General Meeting at the Home Office. The photograph includes the Home Secretary, the Rt. Hon. Sir W. Joynson-Hicks, Bt., M.P., Sir Leonard Dunning, H.M. Inspector of Constabulary and President of the PMAS, Captain S. A. Wood, the Secretary, and Chief Inspector B. D. Pinkerton, Chairman

which continued to make the PMAS highly attractive as it headed for its first Quinquennial Valuation.

At that time, the PMAS was evaluated every five years; its assets, investments, rates of interest, management costs and every aspect of its financial operations were to be scrutinised as a means of ensuring that it provided only the best, that its rules and procedures were being adhered to, and that its affairs were being properly managed. The man chosen to undertake that first evaluation was Mr J. Murray Laing, FIA, FFA, now the Society's Consulting Actuary. He presented his report at the 1927 Annual Meeting which was held in the St Mungo Hall, Glasgow, the first time the Society had met in Scotland. Coincidentally, Glasgow was Mr Murray Laing's home town.

Without going into the detail of his speech at that meeting, he did report that the position was then excellent, and that the Society had revealed a remarkable achievement.

Sir Leonard Dunning

He paid tribute to the founding officers, to the Home Office for its unstinting support, and to Sir Leonard Dunning for the vital role he had played in its steady success.

By adding together the surplus in each of the Society's funds, there was a total surplus of more than £10,000 after five years of operation; this was in spite of depreciation of some assets due to the effects of the General Strike, and Mr Murray Laing put forward his proposals for the disposal of the surplus to benefit members – one idea was to reduce the premiums of those aged over 65 in the Whole Life Section. There were then 1,780 such members and they gained a reduction of two pence in the shilling (one sixth) for the rest of their lives. A shilling was equivalent to the modern 5p, while an old penny was then one twelfth of a shilling.

The annual income of the PMAS from premiums at the end of 1926 was £40,481; members had taken out a total of 15,967 policies and the total amount assured had risen to just over £1 million. Funds, as disclosed on the balance sheet, totalled £121,657. It was a magnificent achievement – as Mr Murray Laing said, further arguments should be unnecessary to convince the country's police officers that membership of the PMAS was in their own best interests. And to add gloss to that report, the hardworking secretary, Captain Wood, had been making his own efforts to make the occasion even more memorable. At the close of the previous year's business, membership of the Endowment Fund totalled 9,283.

He set out to raise that figure to 10,000 by the end of that meeting – policies were sold during the actual conference and before it concluded, Captain Wood could report reaching that significant figure.

It was a splendid Annual Meeting which produced tremendous faith in the PMAS and led to an even wider interest in its benefits.

Wales was host to the Society for the first time in 1928 when the seventh Annual Meeting was held at Cardiff. It was reported that premiums for pensioners aged 65 and over had been reduced as earlier proposed and the healthy situation raised the question as to whether any similar form of relief could be directed towards members of the former PMAA. Their present contributions were heavier than those formerly paid to that Association. No firm decision was made because such relief must depend upon the success of future operations, but the Chief Constable of South Shields, Mr W. Scott, did suggest concessions be made for those who had been paying contributions for more than 55 years! The Chairman then had to explain that the funds of the Whole Life Branch were quite separate from those of the Endowment Branch; it was the Endowment Branch which was in such a strong position but its funds could not be touched for the benefit of members of the Whole Life Branch, ie, those who had transferred from the old PMAA.

At that stage, the PMAS still administered only those two types of insurance, ie the Whole Life Branch which was restricted to members of the old Police Mutual Assurance Association, and the Endowment Branch which had been created by the new PMAS for serving police officers and their wives.

Some members began to wonder if there was scope for additional forms of insurance within the PMAS. As early as 1925, the Chief Constable of Oxford, Mr Fox, had asked whether the Society should consider endowment policies specifically for children of police officers but this had been rejected. The reason was that it was possible, under the existing rules, to arrange PMAS insurance in a child's name and for

POLICE MUTUAL ASSURANCE SOCIETY.

MEETING AT WINCHESTER.

A well-attended meeting was held in Winchester on the 13th inst., to explain to members of the City Force the advantages offered by the Endowment Scheme of the P.M.A.S. The Chief Constable, Mr. W. G. Stratton, presided, and the gathering was addressed by Captain S. A. Wood, Secretary to the Society.

CAPTAIN WOOD, who was introduced by the Chief Constable, expressed his pleasure at being afforded an opportunity of speaking at Winchester. Unfortunately, the P.M.A.S. only had one policy holder in the City Force, but he hoped that when the position occupied by the Society had been explained many officers would desire to become policy holders. The business of the Society, from the date it commenced operations, had been conducted on actuarial lines, and the first quinquennial valuation disclosed a thoroughly sound position. He was glad to say that investments to date exceeded, at cost price, the sum of £170,000, and over 12,000 certificates were now in force in the Endowment Branch. Having regard to the remarkable progress made during the first six and a half years, and the present favourable situation, his committee felt justified in predicting a future of great expansion and prosperity. The Secretary then proceeded to explain the Endowment Scheme in detail.

THE CHIEF CONSTABLE expressed to Captain Wood the thanks of the meeting. He (Mr. Stratton) was quite sure all those present had listened with interest to the Secretary's address and would give the matter careful consideration.

such policies to mature when the child was 14 or 15; already many parents were making use of that system. The question of special insurance for children of police officers was raised once more at the 1930 Annual Meeting and again rejected; it was said that the finest way for an officer to make provision for his family was to insure his own life.

In 1927, however, another idea was proposed. It was suggested that the PMAS should consider the granting of pensions to widows of police officers, such pensions being supplementary to those already available under the Police Pensions Act of 1921. The proposal was taken seriously and the Society asked its Consulting Actuary, Mr J. Murray Laing, to examine the feasibility of such a scheme.

His careful calculations were considered at the 1928 meeting in Cardiff by which time the Society had again been asked for details of any such scheme. But the Actuary's report was not favourable, one aspect being that contributions would have to be very high, and the PMAS could not consider any scheme under which a flat rate of premium would be charged regardless of the entry age.

And suppose a wife did take out such a pension scheme and then died before her husband? The Actuary pointed out that in such a case, all her contributions would be forfeited to the Society. The Management Committee did consider all the merits and all the risks attached to such a proposal, but Chief Inspector Pinkerton, in his role of Chairman of the Management Committee, felt the Society would not be justified in undertaking this scheme, partly because of the high premiums that were necessary but also because of other financial risks involved. It was said, however, that if every police force in the country was in favour of the PMAS undertaking widows' pensions, then the Management Committee would further explore the possibility. Such backing was never received.

The discussion which ensued highlighted various other schemes still operating within police forces; some did cater for widows and orphans of police officers, but having listened to the clear warnings given by the Actuary during his submission, many chief constables began to worry about the financial viability of their own force schemes.

Very few, it transpired, were actuarially sound and the Chief Constable of Staffordshire, Lieutenant-Colonel H.P. Hunter, said that the PMAS must not be drawn into any scheme not based on sound business lines – the PMAS must not be considered on the lines of benevolence; it was a business and had to be administered in a business-like manner!

It was this professional attitude which had, even by this early stage, placed the PMAS on such a sound footing; in fact, in 1929, Captain Wood said it was in an unassailable position. It was now represented in every force in England except six, every police force in Wales was represented but 23 tiny Scottish forces were not. For the first time in its history, the income from weekly premiums now exceeded £1,000 and the Society's funds exceeded £200,000.

Sir Herbert Hunter

In spite of this continuing success, less than a third of all police officers had become members (18,000 out of 65,000 officers) and this caused the President, Sir Leonard Dunning, to wonder why the others had not joined. In his opening address at the 1929 conference in Great Yarmouth, he asked, "I wonder if the policeman of today is saving money as he ought?"

He then said this, *"I know he is spending money and I think he is spending much of it wisely. I see it in the higher standard of living. I see in the married men's houses the better furniture, the better clothes and food. I see in the single men's quarters the trouser presses and boot trees which are signs of a higher standard of personal comfort and success – a few more rungs up the ladder of social position. The motor bikes, motor cars and the expensive perambulators are means of travel to which the old-time policeman could not aspire. But is some of that money being put away for the future?"*

He gave examples of young constables dying and leaving

widows and young children and his stirring speech at that meeting asked for a change of mood among young policemen – he wanted a mood of thrift. In fact, he called it a duty – he described it as *'the imperative duty of thrift'*. He earnestly asked young policemen to think about their future and pointed out that the PMAS offered terms unequalled by any of the great industrial insurance companies. A couple of years later, Sir Leonard was to repeat this warning – he advised young constables to beware of the tremendous temptations of buying expensive goods like wireless sets, motor cycles and clothes on the instalment system. He felt it was far wiser to save up the full amount before committing oneself to a purchase – better even, he said, was the notion of putting the equivalent of such instalments into the secure hands of the PMAS! That would make more money!

One approach in 1929 was to persuade their wives to urge membership of the PMAS and Sir Leonard's own wife, Lady Dunning, set an example at the 1929 meeting by becoming a member. At the same meeting, it was announced that the redoubtable Chairman of the Management Committee, Chief Inspector Pinkerton, had been promoted to Superintendent.

Thus the PMAS entered the 1930s in a buoyant mood, albeit tinged with some anxiety about the future.

That anxiety was due to reports of financial uncertainties in the USA and in the UK, one result of which was to reduce, for the first time, the value of the Society's investments. Gilt-edged securities had suddenly dropped in value in December 1929, but had recovered; furthermore, 1929 had, for some reason, been a year of an unduly high number of deaths, a state which affected all insurance companies. The finances of the Society were therefore scrutinised with a high degree of caution and it was felt that the PMAS could withstand any likely pressures from unexpected fluctuations in the stock market. The PMAS had no need to sell any of its investment stock for example, and any depreciation would be revealed in the accounts. Such a depreciation would be a 'paper' reduction and would remain so unless the stocks were sold or the investments realised.

It is interesting, in light of the 1990–91 privatisation schemes, to learn that some of the investments of the PMAS in the 1930s were in debentures, preference shares, ordinary shares and stocks of the companies which then provided gas, water, electric light and power, as well as some in the docks, harbours and drainage boards and undertakings of that time.

At the 1931 Annual Meeting, Sir Leonard Dunning announced his retirement from the post of HM Chief Inspector of Constabulary, but was retained by the PMAS as its President.

One of his actions at that meeting, which was in Portsmouth, was to send a telegram of loyal greetings to the King and Queen who were, that morning, visiting the town's dockyards. The telegram was duly sent from "the members of the Police Mutual Assurance Society of England, Scotland and Wales" and it resulted in a response from their Majesties. They sent their good wishes to the PMAS and its members and this was probably the first direct link between the Society and members of the Royal Family. Other associations were to follow.

The ninth Annual General Meeting, Edinburgh, 1930

BACK ROW   No.2.Sub.Insp.L.Kerr,Liverpool; 4.Mr.W.Southwell,Salford; 6.Insp.H.J.Deane,Birmingham; 7.P.C. H.Harrison,Birmingham; 9. Ch.Insp.G.R.Goldsmith,Northampton; 10.Lt.Col.H.P.Hunter,O.B.E. C.C. Staffordshire; 12.P.C. L.R.Stephens, Plymouth; 13.Insp.J.R.Stansfield,Salford; 16.Mr.C.Walker, M.B.E. Lanarkshire.

MIDDLE ROW   Nos.3. to 11 - Insp.G.W.Mynors,Nottingham; P.C. T.Simpkins,Luton; Mr.C.R.Fox, C.C. Oxford; Mr.F.W.Myers, D.C.C. Leics; Supt.W.Cartwright, Derby; Mr.A.W.Hopkins, D.C.C. Gloucestershire; Mr.P.D.Keep, C.C. Neath; Mr.G.S.Staunton, M.B.E. A.C.C. East Suffolk; Mr.T.Davies, C.C. Portsmouth.

FRONT ROW   Supt A.F.Low (Authorised Officer,Edinburgh); Capt.S.A.Wood (Secretary); Mr.C.J.L.Hickling (Hon Tres); Mr.J.Murray Laing, F.I.A. F.F.A. (Consulting Actuary); Mr.R.Ross, C.B.E. M.V.O. C.C. Edinburgh, (Vice Pres); Supt.B.D.Pinkerton, Birmingham (Chairman of Committee); Sir Leonard Dunning (President); Lt.Col.W.D.Allan. O.B.E. H.M. Inspector for Scotland (Trustee); Mr.C.C.H.Moriarty, O.B.E. A.C.C. Birmingham, (Trustee); Mr.W.H.Newton, F.C.A. (Auditor); Mr.F.H.Mardlin, Northampton; Mr.T.M.Harris, Wakefield; Mr.E.E.Dalton, Leeds.

One vexed question that began to arise around this time was the payment of expenses for Authorised Officers when attending the Annual Meeting. They received absolutely nothing for their work which had, without doubt, enabled the PMAS to establish itself in such a positive manner, and from time to time subsequent meetings did hear voices raised about the question of expenses for travelling and subsistence. The topic had been discussed at the 1927 meeting and rejected. In 1931, it was again discussed. Ex-Superintendent E.E. Dalton of Leeds City Police suggested that some form of assistance be given to delegates when attending the annual meetings, but the Society's Management Fund, operating on such a narrow percentage margin, did not have the money for such expenses. The suggestion was not entirely ruled out, however, but on that occasion it was impossible to authorise expense payments. All surplus funds, less the basic costs incurred in managing the Society, were passed over for benefits to be paid to members.

The Society did say that when money could be put aside for delegates' expenses, then it would be done.

Meanwhile, the Society was progressing with remarkable confidence. Each year, its membership was increasing by about 2,000 and in 1930, despite the effects of the recession, the Society's investments were increased – in that year, they exceeded £300,000. Their investment portfolio showed some adventurous trends because the Society had now invested some £20,000 in Australian securities. But Australia, like the UK and America, was undergoing its financial setbacks and the value of the Australian holdings dwindled. But the Society did not panic – instead of selling those investments, it decided to retain them in the knowledge that they would, in time, regain any lost values.

Another factor aired at the 1931 meeting was that the Society would soon have to pay money to those who had, in the very beginning, taken out 10-year policies. Those policies would soon mature and so a large amount would have to be paid to those policyholders. The question of bonus payments would be discussed nearer the time and, of course, now that the Society was approaching the completion of its first 10 years of operation, it would also be subjected to its second Quinquennial Valuation.

It was acknowledged that 1930–31 had produced the most anxious period of the Society's ten-year history; unprecedented depreciation of investments had affected every investor, large and small, but the PMAS had survived and in fact their investments had made a full recovery by 15th March 1932. This recovery was reported at the 1932 Annual Meeting held at the Home Office in the presence of Sir Russell Scott, the Permanent Under-Secretary of State for Home Affairs who was deputising for the Home Secretary. That year's meeting reported continuing expansion – an increase in members with surpluses in the management fund, the Whole Life Fund and the Endowment Assurance Fund, and the payment of permanent bonuses in the Endowment Scheme.

The story was one of continuing success and at this stage it is interesting to note that the officers remained unchanged – Sir Leonard Dunning was still President, Superintendent Pinkerton was still Chairman of the Management Committee, Mr J. Murray Laing was still the Consulting Actuary and Captain S.A. Wood continued in his important role as the prudent, fastidious secretary. Lloyds remained as the Society's bankers and Mr C.C.H. Moriarty continued as one of the original trustees. It was a remarkable team even though membership of the Management Committee, an elected body, had undergone a few changes.

This rock-firm progress of the PMAS now contrasted vividly with the uncertainties of the police service itself. The suggested employment of women as police officers was causing a fuss; they had earlier been employed by the Metropolitan Police but had been disbanded in 1921.

The Police Federation, under the chairman of its Joint Central Committee, Sergeant Holmes, said that the work expected to be done by policewomen could be done by police matrons. The

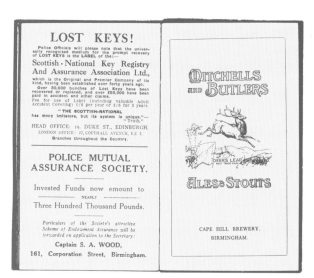

Extract from 1931 PMAS diary

Federation saw no cause to employ women as police officers. But when they were recruited, there was horror when the Federation said they should receive the same pay as male officers, and there was further uproar when a Select Committee proposed the abolition of the smaller borough forces. They recommended that all non-county borough forces operating in areas with a population of less than 30,000, should merge with the appropriate counties. But there was worse – as part of the austerity measures being suffered by the whole nation, the police had to endure a cut in their pay. The Federation found itself fighting a range of important battles, including the welfare of police widows, and these struggles continued.

For the PMAS, it was time for its second Quinquennial Valuation and this, plus the annual reports of 1932 and 1933, gave every reason to be confident of the future. Assets of the PMAS had reached £500,000 and membership was constantly increasing and by the end of 1933, the total income for the Society was more than £90,000 per annum.

The 1934 Annual Meeting was held in the Police Headquarters at Newcastle-upon-Tyne and once again, the Society found itself closely linked with police history. Their host was Mr F. J. Crawley, the Chief Constable of Newcastle City Police and he was known for his police invention – it was the police box. His idea was then in use throughout the country and so established an important means of communication between officers on the beat and their headquarters or divisional offices. At that meeting, as in several earlier ones, the question of expenses being paid to delegates and authorised officers was raised, but the Society felt the expenditure would be too heavy for its limited management fund.

The 1935 meeting in Brighton was notable for several reasons. One was that the Society sent a telegram to the King and Queen upon the celebration of their Silver Jubilee, and received a reply from His Majesty. Another memorable fact was that ladies were present – these were not police women, however, but the ladies of some of the officers who were attending and they were members in their own right. At this, Sir Leonard said he could now realise one of his ambitions – he could open the meeting with the words "Ladies and Gentlemen"! Also commented upon at this meeting were the benefits of the annual meeting making use of venues around the country for its assemblies.

This alone served as a recruiting campaign because policies were sold at each annual meeting, and the fact that the PMAS, a national society, chose to meet in places as varied as local town halls, police headquarters, hotels and even the Home Office did introduce its work to an increasing number of potential members. At that meeting, the Chief Constable of Brighton, Captain W. J. Hutchinson and Mrs Hutchinson, both became members! And the annual income of the PMAS now reached £100,000.

Another factor was that on 1st July 1935, police pay would be restored to its former rate – half had been reinstated in July 1934, and the rest would follow this year and the Society saw this as an opportunity for yet more officers to invest that modest increase of 5% in the PMAS. This must have had some effect because the following annual meeting in Harrogate heard that the annual income had risen to £112,463 and that assets now exceeded £600,000. They had risen from £300,000 in 1932 to double that figure within four years. A year later, the assets had risen to £700,000 and it became Mr Pinkerton's dream to have the Society's assets reach the significant figure of £1 million. Even at this stage, however, it was an astonishing success story, and the same team of officials was guiding the Society along its highly successful route. There were still only two sections – the Whole Life which was restricted to members of the old PMAA and the Endowment

Scheme for serving officers and their wives.

Then Sir Leonard Dunning's health failed. For the first time, he missed an annual meeting and promptly announced his impending retirement as President. It was the seventeenth annual meeting, and it was held in Hull on 17th June 1938. The story which unfolded at that meeting was one of still further success with increased investments and more policies plus a confident forecast that the Society's assets would shortly reach £1 million.

Overall progress was described as 'vigorous' but this meeting signified the beginning of several changes. One was the retirement of Sir Leonard Dunning, a highly respected and much loved President. With his departure, the Society was to lose one of its key figures, a man who had quietly but firmly helped in the very foundation of the PMAS and who had guided it from somewhat shaky beginnings through a period of consolidation to the substantial business that it had now become. Upon his retirement, he was presented with a silver cigarette case bearing the signatures of the members of committee and the officers of the Society, and Lady Dunning was given a cut glass bowl. In return, the Society was pleased to receive a portrait of Sir Leonard; he had been President from 1922 until 1938, a remarkable achievement.

His Vice President was Mr Roderick Ross, CVO, CBE, JP, the former Chief Constable of Edinburgh who had also witnessed the end of the PMAA, but upon his nomination for the office of President he stood down in favour of another man.

The man who therefore replaced Sir Leonard Dunning was a former Chief Constable and a current HM Inspector of Constabulary. He was Lieutenant Colonel, later Sir, Frank Brook, DSO, MC. He was in close touch with every police force in the country and was an ideal choice. Mr Ross remained as Vice President, having said he had joined the old PMAA more than 53 years earlier!

Another major worry was forced upon the Society by the threat of impending war. The terrible effects of the First World

War upon the fortunes of the old Police Mutual Assurance Association were not forgotten, but if a second world war did break out, then there would be a reduction in the numbers of police recruits as well as casualties among police officers. It seemed that history might repeat itself. Many policemen would be called upon to fight as members of HM Forces and casualties among them could result in substantial payments from the Society. This would be aggravated by a halt to recruiting which would reduce the annual income. The Society's officers pondered over the demise of the PMAA whose failure after World War I had resulted in the birth of the modern Police Mutual.

The last annual meeting before the war was at Bournemouth in 1939 where it was mentioned that the PMAS expenditure was a mere 3% of income, well within the permitted 5%. At this time, with assets of £1 million in sight, the PMAS diary was proving very popular but there was concern at the low PMAS membership within some forces, Hampshire in particular.

In spite of the political situation, efforts to recruit new members would continue but it was decided that no annual meetings would be held during hostilities. The Bournemouth meeting would be the last for several years, although meetings of the Committee of Management would continue, and Special General Meetings would be held from time to time. The fourth Quinquennial Valuation, due in 1942, was also deferred.

It may be significant, however, that the number of policies issued during the first nine months of 1939, the year war broke out, was greater than the total for the corresponding period in any previous year. But because of the risks attached to police officers who might be called to join HM Forces for the duration of the war, no proposals were accepted from police officers described as 'of fighting age'. However, First Police War Reserves would be accepted as members and in 1942, policewomen were accepted on the same terms as men, but only if application was made within six months of the date any policewoman was passed for service by a police surgeon. Applications from members of the Women's Auxiliary Police Corps, however, were not accepted.

It was not possible, under the Society's rules, to grant a contract excluding war risks, but the rules were amended on 5th July 1940 and special conditions were incorporated for police officers at risk from hostilities. The immediate effect was that 800 new policies were issued, but by the end of 1940, the number of deaths of PMAS members due to war operations was 25.

The advent of war was already having its effect on the thriving PMAS. One of its Committee of Management was called up – he was E.B. Brereton but he was to survive; he later returned to Staffordshire as a Chief Inspector. But the call-up of serving police officers did result in some changes to the Society's procedures – collection of contributions from police officers serving in HM Forces had to be considered, as did non-payment of premiums by prisoners of war or those listed as missing on active service. All cases were considered with sympathy and in one case, the sum assured was paid to the widow of a policeman who died while he was a prisoner of war.

There were other more mundane matters to consider, such as insuring the Society's own office equipment against war damage, and photographing a range of important documents, then storing them securely to prevent loss from enemy action.

Before the end of 1940, and in spite of the war, the assets of the PMAS had reached the magic figure of £1 million. The precise figure was £1,036,384 8s. 10d. – Pinkerton's dream had come true and he continued as Chairman of the Management Committee even though he had by then retired from Birming-

Mr. F. J. Crawley the host Chief Constable to the PMAS Conference at Police Headquarters, Newcastle-upon-Tyne in 1934 invented the police box which is illustrated on the front of this Ladybird Book

ham City Police.

It was during the war that the Society lost its faithful Vice President, Mr Ross. He died in 1943 and his successor was Mr C.C.H. Moriarty, CBE, BA, LLD, now Chief Constable of Birmingham.

He was also a Senior Moderator, Large Gold Medallist and Prizeman in History, Law and Political Economy of Trinity College, Dublin, as well as author of the famous Moriarty's *Police Law*. He remained a trustee of the Society.

After the war, the Society's annual meetings resumed. The first after the war, but the 19th in sequence, was held on 7th June 1946 at the Home Office. As the Chairman said in his opening remarks, "*Much has happened since the last AGM in Bournemouth!*"

The war was over and it was time to look forward to greater changes, both within the Society and within the police service. As the PMAS was seeking to expand its interests, so the British police service was about to undergo many alterations. At the end of the war, for example, some 12,000 officers were still serving in the armed forces and they were expected to rejoin their constabularies during the summer of 1946, and so the war-time restrictions on resignation and retirement of serving officers were lifted. But instead of increasing the number of serving police, this led to a massive exodus of older officers before the end of 1945, many of whom were war reserves, and so a recruiting drive was launched.

The Home Office said that 10,000 officers would be required over the next two years, and it established District Training Schools to cater for the influx. These were later to prove a huge asset to the PMAS in the 1950s when it adopted the policy of visiting these centres to address recruits.

But the anticipated recruits did not join – there were better wages in industry and commerce, police housing was shoddy, police working conditions were poor, split shifts were operated and there was a high level of resignations.

Combined with the lack of suitable recruits, the manpower

situation was causing concern at all levels. Added to this concern was the upheaval of amalgamation of some police forces. Although certain forces had been amalgamated during the war under the Defence Regulations, this was purely a war-time facility, but when hostilities ended the Home Secretary took the opportunity to implement earlier recommendations that the smaller non-county borough forces should be compulsorily amalgamated with larger forces. The Police Act, 1946 brought this about; as a consequence, 45 non-county borough police forces were merged with the surrounding counties, five voluntary amalgamation schemes were made, five compulsory orders were made and one county borough, which had never had its own police force, was suddenly allowed to have one. That was Bournemouth. The only non-county borough force to avoid these amalgamations was Cambridge.

Thus within the space of a few months, the entire police service of this country had been radically altered and a new professionalism was about to emerge. Some forces, for example, took the opportunity to change their method of paying police officers' wages – they would be paid by cheque instead of the usual packet of cash being handed over on a pay parade.

And with this system, there came the practice of deducting funds from pay – this could be done by the County or City Treasurers and so the PMAS found itself benefiting from this new system. Instead of the old method of Authorised Officers collecting premiums in cash and paying them over to the Society, it could now be done through the banking organisations. (See the section on 'Authorised Officers', page 207).

These and other changes were to prove of everlasting benefit to the PMAS. It was already considering changes of its own – should it be able to lend money to police officers on the security of their own houses? It was decided that no action should be taken on that proposal, but changes were being made. A modest advertising campaign began, a new table of sums assured was produced, bonuses were discussed and the combined result of this was that money poured into the Society as new members enrolled.

It is not surprising that, by 1947, (and in spite of the adverse effects of the war) its assets were heading for the £1.5 million mark and there was a steady annual increase in the number of new policies being issued. Following the war, the PMAS was stronger than ever and there can be little doubt that part of this success was because police officers were happy to allow small deductions at source from their pay. If the deductions were made before they received their money, they did not miss them.

Most of them accepted that "What you've never had, you never miss", and so deductions from pay at source became a splendid incentive for saving and a popular means of paying subscriptions to the PMAS, as well as to other clubs and societies.

At the 20th Annual Meeting in Blackpool in 1947, Sir Frank Brook announced that the assets of the PMAS had reached £1.5 million and that membership exceeded 36,000. Mr Murray Laing compared this with the first year of operation when the Society had an overdraft of £2,000 and had been warned by the Home Office that 5,000 members were needed to make the PMAS a viable concern. Mr Murray Laing added that this success had exceeded anything that he might have anticipated – and the Society celebrated by buying a new typewriter for the office!

As the first fifty years of the century drew to a close, therefore, the PMAS found itself in a very strong and thriving position with an annual income in the region of £150,000 and assets worth ten times that amount. It had increased its sum assured on one life from £350 to £500 and at this stage it was realised that more staff were needed. In 1949, it was decided to appoint an assistant secretary.

His name was J.W. Hadley.

CHAPTER 3

A PERIOD
OF ADVANCEMENT
1950 – 1967

John Hadley's introduction to the PMAS came through an advertisement in the insurance press. It sought applications for the post of Assistant Secretary to a very specialised assurance society which catered exclusively for police officers. It was called the Police Mutual Assurance Society. At the time, Mr Hadley was working for Wesleyan and General Insurance as deputy head of its investment department; he had been with the company for eighteen years and there is no doubt that a worthwhile future awaited.

But John Hadley was restless; after war service, he wanted a challenge and a new direction. He made enquiries about the post and learned that the appointment would be made with the intention that the successful applicant would succeed the incumbent secretary, the fastidious but competent Captain Wood. When Hadley saw the premises in which he would work, however, he almost failed to apply. In his own words, "When I did a quick recce of the office at 161 Corporation Street, Birmingham, I found what can be only described as Dickensian squalor – it was shabby, down-at-heel and most unattractive."

Nonetheless, he did sense a whiff of excitement and a challenge and he could appreciate the potential of what was then a little-known assurance society.

He applied – and he was successful. It was the start of an association which was to continue for more than a quarter of a century, during which time John Hadley progressed to become the Society's Manager & Secretary, and in which the PMAS positively established itself,

John Hadley in his office at 161 Corporation Street, Birmingham — "That damned garret!"

particularly among the police officers it served.

The first months of John Hadley's work with the PMAS, however, did not give him the challenge he sought – instead, he found himself in a sanatorium in the Cotswolds fighting an advanced tuberculosis infection in his right lung. The treatment required six months off work, hardly the most auspicious beginning for a new member of staff. There is little doubt that, at this stage, he regarded himself as a very poor prospect and he wondered whether the PMAS would keep the post open for his return – if and when that occurred.

The Society did. At a meeting of the Committee of Management in January 1950, it was decided to grant full pay to Mr Hadley for the first three months of his absence (with effect from 1st December 1949), and half pay for the succeeding three months. Happily, the news from the sanatorium was good and at the April 1950 meeting of the Management Committee, Mr Hadley attended to give a report on his progress. The Committee lifted his spirits by saying they would welcome him back to the office as soon as he had a clear certificate from his doctor.

But in the few weeks that he had worked with the PMAS before his illness, John Hadley had operated with decisiveness and speed. Many forces were still operating the old pay parades and collecting voluntary deductions in cash. Mr Hadley decided to attend those parades to see how they functioned and he learned that many did not have the presence of a PMAS Authorised Officer. He then sent a questionnaire to all police forces to obtain precise information about their methods of pay and their systems for making deductions.

During his long illness, and fortified with the knowledge he had already acquired, he gave a lot of thought to improving the basic links between Britain's police forces and the PMAS.

In his enforced absence from the activity of the office, he had time to study the results of his questionnaires and when he returned to the office, fully fit, he was bursting with ideas. Three main factors had presented themselves to him:

(a) the PMAS had only scratched the surface so far as potential members were concerned. Fewer than 50% of the 70,000 British officers were members.

(b) an authorised officer was required in every force. That was vital if any real progress was to be made.

(c) All police forces should be encouraged to deduct PMAS premiums from officers' pay. This was based on the premise that you don't miss what you don't get, so it should encourage new members to join.

John Hadley wanted to approach all chief constables with a request that they endeavour to implement his ideas about authorised officers and pay deductions, but in presenting this proposal to the austere and somewhat conservative Captain Wood, Mr Hadley was unsure of his reaction. After all, Captain Wood had guided the PMAS from a very early stage and here was a newcomer advocating change! Happily, the Captain's response was positive if somewhat guarded and so Mr Hadley began a systematic appeal to all chief constables. Although it took a year or two for every force to appoint its own Authorised Officer, this was eventually achieved and some of the larger forces even appointed Authorised Officers within their divisions. This was a fine start to Mr Hadley's plans.

The practice of deducting premiums from pay was not achieved with such simplicity; not only had chief constables to be in agreement with the innovation, but they had to solicit the co-operation of the nation's county, borough or city treasurers all of whom operated their own systems; many had their own views on such practices and Mr Hadley anticipated some opposition even though a handful of forces were already deducting funds from pay. Consideration had also to be given to police officers themselves. Some police officers were not happy about deductions being made at source from their pay packets, but the Police Federation, recognising the enormous benefits that would accrue to its members and indeed to all police officers, did its best to encourage this breakthrough.

At this time, another factor was working for the benefit of the PMAS. The Home Office had recently established District Police Training Centres throughout the country and, after being approached by the PMAS, a meeting of their Commandants agreed that representatives of the PMAS could periodically address the students. The Society had specified that the emphasis would be upon the fact that the PMAS was *their* society, run by police officers for police officers.

These developments, plus an advertising campaign which asked "Have YOU got the MAXIMUM with the MUTUAL?" and "You might live without insurance, but DON'T die without it", produced a massive surge of new business. Police officers began to talk with pride about their very own insurance company as they began to appreciate the benefits of wise investment.

Following these changes in the early 1950s, the PMAS found itself facing further alterations – Mr C.C.H. Moriarty who had been such a stalwart in its early days, now resigned as Vice President and another sturdy supporter, the indefatigable Ben Pinkerton missed the 1951 Annual General Meeting due to illness – but he was back in action for the August 1951 Committee of Management meeting. Nonetheless, that illness warned the Committee of Management that its old and highly successful team may soon face enforced changes. It was also in 1951 that PMAS assets rose to £1,750,000, with some 36,000 certificate holders being registered.

This represented a third of the strength of the British police service – so it left two thirds to be recruited to membership, a daunting task. It was clear that other means of making police officers aware of the PMAS and its benefits had to be employed. One idea was the reprinting of the PMAS diary, abandoned during the war years; it was suggested that plans be made to issue the diary beginning with the year 1953 but careful examination of printing costs revealed that it would incur a considerable loss. The

WILL YOU SEE **YOUR** NAME HERE

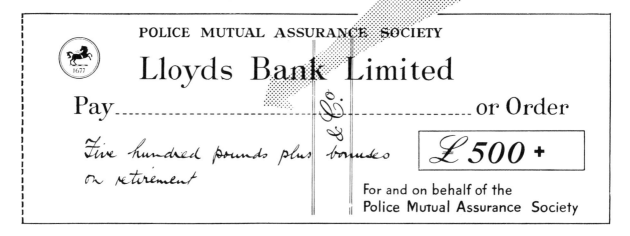

POLICE MUTUAL ASSURANCE SOCIETY

Lloyds Bank Limited

Pay.. or Order

Five hundred pounds plus bonuses on retirement

$£500+$

For and on behalf of the
Police Mutual Assurance Society

IT'S NEVER TOO LATE
TO DO YOURSELF
A GOOD TURN

BY MAKING SURE YOU HAVE

THE MAXIMUM IN THE 'MUTUAL'

MAXIMUM £500 TO ANY ONE MEMBER
£1,000 TO HUSBAND-AND-WIFE
(all on the life of the husband if desired)

ASK YOUR LOCAL AUTHORISED OFFICER FOR DETAILS

★ **YOU CAN'T DO BETTER** ★

POLICE MUTUAL ASSURANCE SOCIETY

Secretary: Mr. J. W. Hadley, F.C.I.I.

Registered Office: 10 Greenfield Crescent, Edgbaston, Birmingham, 15

PMAS was still obliged to operate its management expenses within 5% of revenue and although it was functioning at 4% it was felt that the expense of printing some 16,000 copies would be too great. It was decided not to proceed with the PMAS diary, but to advertise in another diary, the one being produced by the *Police Review.*

A similar proposal in 1952 was to print pamphlets which would aid police officers in the performance of their duties. One was *"Ages Prescribed by Law"* and the other was *"Useful Definitions for Police Officers".* This type of information had earlier been printed in the PMAS diary, but the new idea was to issue the information as handy little booklets to recruits at District Police Training Centres. The *"Ages Prescribed by Law"* booklet was not approved, but the *"Useful Definitions"* was sanctioned and since that time, generations of police officers have been grateful for this most convenient means of making important information available to them.

The book of definitions was small enough to be carried on duty within a police officer's notebook or wallet and was universally welcomed. It is still issued, albeit in a slightly larger format.

In considering the costs of such publicity, the PMAS was always aware that its management costs were considerably lower than other assurance societies; some companies' costs were as high as 14% of revenue but the PMAS continued to operate well within the 5% margin. Even so, its progress was impressive and it was considered a far better investment than the smaller benevolent societies still being operated within some forces. It was at this time that the management committee of the Lancashire Constabulary Provident Fund floated a suggestion that the PMAS might wish to absorb that fund and so cater for all its members. But after some deliberation by the PMAS Committee of Management, the proposal was not proceeded with, although it was a reminder that small benevolent societies which still existed could not compete with the PMAS in terms of security and investment expertise. This

Opposite Early advertisement — a facsimile of a cheque which formed part of an advertisement in 1932 near-merger was a reminder that some similar societies had earlier regarded the PMAS as a threat to their existence. Was this proposal regarded as a threat, or was it seen as a possible helping hand from a friendly giant? We shall never know.

It was in 1951 that Sir Frank Brook, the President, said that the PMAS echoed the words of the popular song, Old Man River because 'it just kept rolling along' while its benefits kept spreading and deepening, but in fact changes were ahead. In the year that followed, a small change occurred in the procedure for making application for a PMAS certificate of membership.

The rules were relaxed and it meant that, in some cases, membership of the endowment scheme could now be obtained without the formality of a medical examination. Those who could benefit from this change included men and women who had joined the force within the previous two years and whose medical examinations at that time had been satisfactory. The amended procedures also permitted entry without a medical examination to police officers and their wives between the ages of 51 and 60 who took out a ten-year term of assurance, provided that the information on their proposal forms was satisfactory and that the weekly instalment did not exceed two shillings (10p).

But 1952 was to cast several shadows over the Society. One sadness was that it lost two of its most important and faithful workers. One was its actuary, Mr J. Murray Laing who died that year. He had guided the PMAS from its very modest beginnings and his sound advice had ensured its solid, continuing progress from that time.

He was described as a pillar of strength with a delightful personality, and at the Annual General Meeting on 20th June 1952 the delegates stood in silent tribute to his memory. At the same meeting, the indefatigable Chairman of the Committee of Management, Mr B.D. (Ben) Pinkerton resigned due to ill health. He had suffered a serious illness during the previous year and felt it was time to make way for a younger person; he had been Chairman since 1922, a period of thirty astonishingly successful years, and so in 1952 he resigned from all PMAS committees.

In referring to Ben Pinkerton's resignation, the President, Sir Frank Brook, said that Mr Pinkerton was too valuable to the Society for him to carry the burden of its work for too long. He realised that resignation would cause Mr Pinkerton considerable pain, but that with his background, knowledge and experience, the Society could not allow him to fade out entirely! In appreciation of his services, therefore, he was made an Honorary Vice President and an *ex-officio* member of the Committee of Management — which meant he could attend meetings whenever he wished. Sadly, this would not be for long because Mr Pinkerton died within the year. His tremendous contribution to the Society cannot be equalled — his long-held dream of seeing the Society's assets reach a million pounds had been fulfilled during his lifetime and one can merely speculate upon the enormous pride with which he would have viewed its present achievements.

Another shadow over the Society around this period concerned its level of management expenditure. Just before his death, Ben Pinkerton had drawn the attention of the Committee of Management to the increasing levels of expenditure, pointing out that 4% of revenue, although less than the official limit, was no longer adequate. The cost of the quinquennial valuation, new stationery and a loss on the now defunct PMAS diary, plus a reduction in the value of investments, had all contributed to a level of expenditure which was too high and this note of caution was echoed by the Society's auditor.

He was Mr W. H. Newton, MA, FCA, of Newton and Co., Chartered Accountants of Birmingham. At the 1952 Annual General Meeting he said, "The important item before the meeting is the quinquennial valuation which has indeed come out very satisfactorily and is a result of which the members may be very proud. The fall in the market value of the investments was an unavoidable event but the temporary loss is very comfortably covered out of the surplus on the quinquennial valuation, and there is little doubt that the major part of the depreciation in the Endowment Fund will be gradually recovered over the future as the redeemable stock becomes due for payment."

The steady rise in all expenses somewhat upset the balance on the Management Fund which finished with a debit balance of £679. As there was a balance in hand of £687 at the beginning of the year, expenses for valuation and the diary exceeded the four per cent allocation by £1,366.

The auditor went on to suggest that £1,000 be transferred from the surplus which had accrued on previous valuations – in fact, Mr Murray Laing had made this suggestion just before his death and so the transfer of funds was made, with the auditor expressing his confidence that with its continuing increase of funds from premiums, the Society could operate within a four per cent margin in the foreseeable future. His confidence was later to be fully justified.

These setbacks did not halt the continuing progress of the PMAS. A new consulting actuary was appointed – he was Mr Kenneth J. Britt, FIA, FFA, who in recent months had deputised for Mr Murray Laing, while Inspector E.S. Drake of Birmingham City Police was later elected Chairman of the Committee of Management in place of Ben Pinkerton. The PMAS secretary and assistant secretary were now visiting police training centres on a quarterly basis in an attempt to publicise the merits of the Society among recruits, and six new members of the administrative staff at Head Office were appointed to cope with the extra work. And for the security of important documents, a safe was purchased for Head Office! After a short series of setbacks, the Society had gathered itself together and was forging ahead once more.

By 1953, its assets had reached £2,000,000, and steady growth was reported even if the President, Sir Frank Brook said that the PMAS carpet had a few bare patches!

MR E.S. DRAKE,

BEM

Stan Drake was born to a tradition of service. He joined the Royal Army Medical Corps before he was 17, advancing his age a couple of years to do so! He was transferred to the Border Regiment but towards the end of 1916, he was again transferred, this time to the Royal Flying Corps. He had first-hand experience of those early 'flying machines' and remained there until he joined Birmingham City Police in 1923.

He was promoted through the ranks to become Chief Inspector in charge of the Digbeth Sub-Division, an appointment he held until Sir Edward Dodd appointed him staff officer of the Birmingham Special Constabulary in 1958.

Stan Drake was known for having a flair for 'putting things over' in an informative and interesting manner, and he was also respected for his 'unflappability'. He was awarded the British Empire Medal in the 1955 Queen's Birthday Honours List as a recognition of his devotion to the many aspects of the police service with which he had been associated.

Mr Drake was appointed to the General Committee of the PMAS in 1932 and to the Committee of Management in 1937. He was Chairman of the Committee from 1952 until 1969 when he resigned; he was appointed a Life Vice President in recognition of his work for the Society.

Those bare patches were not in the office carpet (the offices in 161 Corporation Street had linoleum floor covering, some of which was renewed in 1951!) but were a descriptive term used by Sir Frank to show that the Society's members, however widespread, by no means fully covered the whole of the UK. Mr W. J. Price, the Chief Constable of Cardiff City Police, the host force for the 1953 meeting, said that if the PMAS was like a carpet with a few bare patches, then Cardiff was one of those patches! His force could muster only about a dozen members, but he excused this by saying that the Cardiff force had its own benevolent society which had been operating for more than 60 years.

Members of the Committee of Management and officers pictured at Cardiff in 1953
Standing (left to right) Mr. K. J. Britt (consulting actuary), Col. Sir Herbert Hunter, Mr. E. J. Dodd,
Mr. W. C. Johnson, Inspector E. S. Drake, Mr. M. B. Hancock (auditor), Mr. H. F. Bill (hon. treasurer)
Seated Mr. C. R. Fox (Vice President), Mr. W. J. Price (CC, Cardiff), Col. Sir Frank Brook, Capt. S. A. Wood

He added, however, that the Cardiff force was fully sympathetic to the aims of the PMAS and urged the Society to work through training schools and convalescent homes to further its recruiting efforts. Inspector Drake responded with an account of the record-breaking progress of the PMAS and there is little doubt that, as a result, several Cardiff officers became new members. This is an example of the benefits to be gained by the Society when visiting differing parts of the UK for its annual meetings but it also revealed that smaller societies continued to function within individual forces.

1954 was to be a year of important changes and one in which another PMAS era came to a close.

Captain Wood decided to retire as secretary of the PMAS after 32 years of impeccable service and John Hadley, now suitably groomed by his worthy predecessor, was appointed in his place. But these changes came at a time of further major developments. Following a visit to the Registry of Friendly Societies by Captain Wood and Kenneth Britt, the Committee of Management decided to form a limited company which would replace the existing trustees of the PMAS. The new company would be known as PMAS Nominees Limited and would be registered under the Companies Act of 1948. At the same time, the number of Vice Presidents would be increased from one to four, the three extra including the three outgoing trustees. Membership of the Nominee Company would be restricted to fourteen, ie the President, four Vice Presidents, the Chairman of the General Committee and eight members of the Committee of Management. All would become directors of the new company, and the rules of the Society were amended to take account of these changes.

By this time, the Society was outgrowing its limited accommodation at 161 Corporation Street in Birmingham, and the Committee of Management decided that it was time to seek new 'more commodious' office premises at a rental not exceeding £1,000 per annum. As the search began, new proposals were discussed by the Society. One was the introduction of a house purchase scheme for police officers.

This would be operated with the co-operation of other financial institutions such as banks, building societies or life assurance companies and would involve life insurance upon the participating police officer and/or his wife. But the idea did not win immediate approval and, because of complications which might arise, plus the limited numbers of staff and restricted office facilities currently tolerated by the Society, it was decided not to proceed with the proposal.

MR JOHN W. HADLEY,
MBE, FCII

John Hadley spent the first eighteen years of his career with the Wesleyan & General Assurance Society. During this time, he served for six years in the Army with the 6th British Armoured Division during the Second World War and saw action in Algeria, Tunisia, Italy and Austria. In May 1949, he emerged from a large field of competitors as the successful candidate for the post of Assistant Secretary of the Police Mutual Assurance Society, and in September 1954 took over from Captain Wood as Secretary. His title was subsequently changed to Manager & Secretary, and he served as the Society's Chief Executive until 1975.

In his early days, Mr Hadley was a very competent light heavyweight boxer, as well as an enthusiastic footballer and hockey player. He gained special recognition as both a hockey umpire and sports administrator. Colleagues say that he was a 'larger-than-life' character who led from the front. His enthusiasm was boundless and he was the ideal leader as the PMAS sought to establish itself in the late 1950s and early 1960s. His service to the police was recognised by the award of the MBE in the 1972 New Year Honours List.

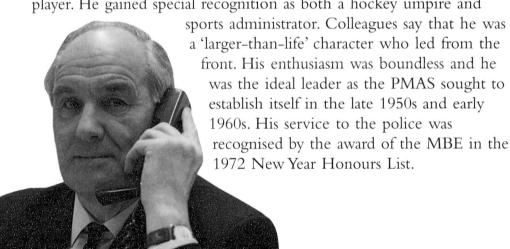

Meanwhile, the PMAS had extended its activities, it had purchased a postal franking machine for its mail and had made some minor changes to its endowment scheme. They affected the paid-up or surrender values of policies, neither being permitted until the policy had been in force for at least one year with 52 paid weekly contributions. The PMAS also sought wider investment powers. Upon the advice of its consulting actuary, it sought and was granted the power to invest in the debentures, mortgage debentures or debenture stock of companies registered in and trading in Great Britain which had a paid-up capital of not less than £500,000.

As if these changes were not enough in one year, the Society did find new premises but not on a rental basis. It purchased a semi-detached house which would be altered to become offices; the cost of purchase was £6,500 and the Society was allowed funds to alter, decorate and furnish the house.

They left their old offices in Corporation Street and it is now a sports shop. The new address was No. 10 Greenfield Crescent, Edgbaston, Birmingham and the staff moved into these premises on Monday 11th October 1954. One of its assets was a large rear garden with a lawn and a rose bed where staff could relax during meal breaks. Shortly before the move, the staff comprised six people – Mr Castledine, Mr Fred Smith, Mrs Latham, Miss Mellor, Miss Baker with Mrs Castledine as a part time typist. The Society would occupy these premises for some sixteen years until it moved into its present accommodation at Alexandra House in Lichfield in 1970.

The 1954 Annual General Meeting was held at Edinburgh and six Scottish Chief Constables attended, along with Mr S. A. Kinnear, HM Inspector of Constabulary for Scotland and Air Vice Marshall R. Graham, CB, CBE, the Commandant of the Scottish Police College. The Vice President of the PMAS, Mr C.R. Fox, Chief Constable of Oxford, deputised for Sir Frank Brook who was in Rome, and welcomed the Scottish guests, saying that in

Some views of the PMAS office at 10 Greenfield Crescent, Edgbaston

England, the District Training Schools welcomed recruitment visits by the PMAS.

He added that he hoped the Scottish Police College would do likewise, and that the Chief Constables present would encourage membership within their own areas. That meeting paid tribute to the work of the retired Captain Wood and made a presentation to him.

From literally nothing, he had built the Society to the point where it had over £2,000,000 of assets and over 300 authorised officers throughout Great Britain. "No organisation," said the Chairman, Inspector E.S. Drake, "could have had a more faithful servant." At the same meeting, the Society's long-time treasurer, Mr H.F. Bill, formerly of Lloyds Bank, also retired and a presentation was likewise made to him.

Later that year, the Society's management staff was increased by the appointment of an assistant secretary, Mr A.F. King, an Associate of the Chartered Insurance Institute and a former wartime pilot. Two further clerks were also recruited. Mr King was to play a very important role within the Society at the side of John Hadley, and these appointments were marked by another milestone in the progress of the PMAS – in 1954, the sum assured under new policies issued that year was more than one million pounds. The precise amount was £1,063,935, and this coincided with a spectacular rise in the value of Stock Exchange securities. In the modest words of Inspector Drake, the Chairman, "1954 was a year of achievement."

In the year that followed, further clerical staff were appointed and authority was given for the assignment of PMAS policies. For example, members may wish to assign the value of their policies to another purpose, perhaps as a gift or as a marriage settlement or even to assist with a mortgage, but after discussion the only assignment permitted was by way of a mortgage.

The Society now decided to increase its range and number of advertisements and it included some in the *Police Review, the Police Chronicle*, the *Police Review Diary* as well as various force magazines and newspapers.

Another factor to consider at this time was officers who were serving in the British Police Contingent in Cyprus. A guerrilla war against the British rule had been started by Greek Cypriots who were seeking 'Enosis', or union with Greece. The conflict involved EOKA, the National Organisation of Cypriot Combatants, and its leaders were the head of the Greek Orthodox Church in Cyprus, Archbishop Makarios, and General Grivas who led the military faction. The risks attached to the police officers serving there were similar to those who had served in World War II, either as members of the armed forces or as police officers at home, but in this case they were police officers serving overseas, albeit without losing their status as British police officers. It was agreed that any claims arising as a result of death from hostilities while serving in Cyprus should be paid in full, without regard to the operation of the usual war risks clause.

At the time of the 29th Annual General Meeting in Harrogate (1956), the Society's assets had reached £2,500,000 and yet there were still some forces who did not permit premiums to be deducted from officers' pay at source, even though many forces had been operating that system for some thirty years!

It was emphasised, however, that this was not the fault of chief constables, for it was usually the city, borough or county treasurers who would not approve of the system. It was pointed out only a year later, however, that 95% of police forces did operate a system of making voluntary deductions from pay for membership of athletic associations and other voluntary societies, of which the PMAS was one.

Among the changes proposed at this time was whether the PMAS could offer further financial services to police officers, such as loans based on the security of their policies. It was pointed out that policies could now be used as security for loans against mortgages or even temporary overdrafts, but that the Committee felt this should not become a general policy. Each case would be dealt with on merit, with special consideration in cases of genuine hardship.

Another question which arose, and which would continue to arise in future years, was whether the Society should issue life assurance policies to pensioners. It was pointed out that many police officers retired about the time of maturity of their policies, and lots had asked if they could replace the maturing policy with another which would operate during their retirement. It was stated that if a police officer took out a policy while still serving, he could continue to pay his premiums while retired, but it was felt that too many problems could be created by extending PMAS facilities to officers who had already retired, even those with existing policies.

Research showed that very few pensioners would make use of the facilities and the administrative work involved was not compatible with any change. The idea, therefore, was not proceeded with and this coincided with an examination of an old rule which allowed Police War Reserves and their wives to obtain policies. The need for that facility had been rendered unnecessary with the passage of time, so it was abolished. There would be no new policies for police war reserves and their wives.

In the early months of 1957, two more valued members of the Society's team announced their retirement. One was Sir Frank Brook, the President, and the other was Mr W. H. Newton, the auditor. Sir Frank was the Society's second President while Mr Newton had been associated with the Society since its inception in 1922. Both had played a major part in the outstanding success of the PMAS and tributes were paid to them and their work. The Society's third President was to be Mr (later Sir) William C. Johnson, CMG, CBE, HM Inspector of Constabulary, with Colonel A. E. Young, the Commissioner of Police for the City of London being elected Vice President in his place. The new auditor was Mr M.B. Hancock of Messrs W. H. Newton and Co., Accountants of Birmingham, thus continuing this firm's long association with the PMAS.

Sir William Johnson

The changes came when the Society was claiming 42,000 police officers as members with a record volume of new business in 1956.

The figure was £2,874,042 for sums assured, with the Society's assets rising to £2,619,620, but in spite of this, only 40% of serving chief constables were members. It was pointed out that Colonel Sir Herbert Hunter, CB, CBE, DL, the former Chief Constable of Staffordshire and a Vice President of the Society, was, at this stage, the only police officer still involved with the PMAS who had been associated with the Society at its very beginning some thirty-five years earlier.

It was a tremendous record and an example to other chief

constables. It was felt that if they joined the Society, then their officers would also be encouraged to become members.

History was made at the 1957 Annual General Meeting in Birmingham with the appointment of the Society's first woman Authorised Officer. She was Woman Sergeant Vera Lee of the North Riding of Yorkshire Constabulary and she was given a warm welcome at the meeting.

Another important event was reported at this meeting. The actuary, Mr Kenneth Britt, referred to the two assurance funds then being operated by the PMAS. The main one was the Endowment Assurance Fund which consisted of the majority of members of the PMAS and it was this fund which was so successful.

The other, the Whole Life Fund, comprised only members of the former Police Mutual Assurance Association who had transferred to the PMAS in 1921. At this stage, more than thirty six years later, that fund had very few members and no possibility of any new ones.

Nonetheless, the two funds were quite separate each with its own investments but in recent years, the Whole Life Fund had had no new money to invest. The prevailing credit squeeze caused its investments to depreciate and it was necessary from time to time to sell investments in order to pay claims. With all securities, even Government ones, showing a loss when they were sold, it had been considered wise to borrow from the Management Fund which had a good balance.

"But," said Mr Britt, "This was only a temporary expedient and it has become obvious that separation of assets will no longer favour the Whole Life Fund."

Upon his recommendation, therefore, the Committee of Management decided that the Whole Life and Endowment Assurance Funds should be amalgamated. No harm would come to the Endowment Assurance Fund through this merger, while it would make a huge beneficial difference to the few remaining Whole Life members. He reminded the meeting that there had always been a strong feeling of goodwill among PMAS members towards members of the old PMAA who had transferred to the PMAS in their time of need. Members of the PMAS has always looked after them, and in the following year, there was another example of that remarkable goodwill. From the end of 1957, all surviving members of the Whole Life Fund would be excused further premiums without reducing sums assured; furthermore, on deaths which occurred at ages over 70, bonuses would be paid in respect of each year by which the age exceeded 70.

It was a remarkable and benevolent gesture towards those old police officers.

This display of traditional PMAS benevolence was, however, overshadowed by some sadness at the loss of an old friend. He was Mr C.C.H. Moriarty whose association with the PMAS could be traced to its very beginnings, and the delegates at the 1958 Annual General Meeting in Folkestone stood in silent tribute to their old colleague. His name lives on, both in the history of this Society and in his famous book Police Law which is still known simply as *Moriarty*.

Apart from this, the 1958 meeting reported another outstanding year with the breaking of four records. Assets had reached £2,864,000; premium income exceeded £500,000 per annum; investment income had reached six figures for the very first time and the Endowment Fund had reached £2,682,678. The Home Secretary sent his congratulations to the meeting, saying that a Society whose assets had rocketed from £15,000 to almost £3m had indeed made a tremendous achievement.

But the Society did not use this opportunity to relax; instead, it embarked on a national publicity campaign designed to recruit even more members. The campaign was in three parts – first, an individual letter outlining PMAS benefits was sent to every police officer in the United Kingdom; second, a poster and leaflet campaign was launched to remind serving officers of the wisdom of investing part of their new pay award, and third, the Society would extend its advertising in police journals so that the name of the PMAS was prominently displayed each week. A special diary was also introduced in 1959 and its success led to a repeat publication in 1960.

In addition to these marketing ideas and the on-going quarterly visits to police training centres by the Secretary and his assistant, the Society decided it would make a direct approach to police forces whose officers had not become members and these included Jersey, the British Transport Police and the Port of London Authority Police. Jersey rejected the idea, saying it already had its own satisfactory insurance scheme and the same reason for rejection was put forward by the Chief Constable of the British Transport Police. In 1959, the Port of London Authority Police did, however, welcome the opportunity for its members to become PMAS members with deduction of premiums being made from pay at source, and it appointed an authorised officer. In the years ahead, both Jersey and the British Transport Police were to change their minds and emulate the PLA Police.

As the 1950s drew to a close, the PMAS had a year of mixed fortunes. At the 1959 Annual General Meeting, there was joy at the news that the value of PMAS assets had increased to £3,333,000, all this money being held in trust for its members. The President, Sir William Johnson, commented that it had taken twenty-one hard and difficult years to reach the first million pounds worth of assets, thirteen years to accumulate the second million, but only three years to record the third million.

As Mr Britt said, "No other comparable institution could show such marked vitality or such splendid progress. There is every reason to believe that the Society will go on from success to success."

One problem facing the Society was the responsibility of being custodian of such large amounts of other persons' money. Sir William said that the money must not be idle, it must be put to work for the benefit of policy holders, but he did add that investment of such funds was at times a real headache. The primary objective was to get security and the second was to achieve a good rate of interest and so the Society's investments were spread across a wide range. He added that the PMAS depended heavily upon the financial acumen of its actuary, Kenneth Britt, and also upon the undoubted skills of its secretary, Mr Hadley. It was at this time that the bank rate had risen to 7% which had depressed the value of the Society's fixed interest-bearing investments, but successive reductions in 1958 had restored the rate to 4%. But when the bank rate was high, the Society had taken the opportunity to invest some of its assets so that benefits would accrue from the higher interest.

Another problem arose because some building societies were refusing to accept PMAS policies as collateral security under their Mortgage Endowment Plan for house purchase. The reason was that the PMAS did not guarantee the special surrender values that were required by the building societies.

The Society was quick to react by effecting a special policy which would guarantee those special values in the future. Several building societies entered a firm working agreement with the PMAS and this was perhaps the prelude to the eventual introduction of the Society's own house purchase scheme which came into effect in 1963.

Among the other matters which surfaced in 1959 was the continuing question of issuing policies to police pensioners but having considered the matter at considerable length, the Committee of Management again decided against it. Another aspect of the Society's concern with older officers was embodied in a special fund known as the Dunning Fund.

As long ago as 1927, Sir Leonard Dunning, the then President of the PMAS, told the Committee of Management that he had appealed, through the police press, for financial help towards a pensioner and wife who could not afford to maintain their PMAS premiums. The old couple had fallen into arrears and their policy had lapsed.

The outcome was that sympathetic readers had sent more than enough money to pay off the arrears and to help the pensioners with future premiums. Sir Leonard had paid the surplus into a bank account so that the money, with interest, could be used to ease similar problems in the future. Between 1927 and 1959, the fund, administered by three trustees, had paid monies to deserving beneficiaries but by the end of 1959 the fund stood at just over £142.

As no further premiums were being collected from members of the Whole Life Section, all such policies were now paid-up, so the need for the Dunning Fund had ceased. After discussion, it was decided to transfer the balance for the benefit of remaining members of the Whole Life Fund.

As the 1950s drew to a close, however, the increased work of the PMAS meant that more accommodation was required but all the available space at No. 10 Greenfield Crescent had been utilised. There was no doubt that the Society's work would expand in the near future and that more office accommodation would be needed, so it was decided to extend the existing premises. The Committee therefore sought an architect to advise the Society and to submit plans but this proposal was not acceptable to the authorities. The extensions could not be carried out and so the PMAS decided to seek a site where they could erect offices more suited to their needs. But in the meantime, the authorities changed their minds because planning permission was approved the following year and the architect, Mr R.L. Stone, outlined his plans for conversion of the existing premises. The conversion would provide accommodation for up to 25 extra clerical staff as well as improved working condi-

Extract from the minutes of a meeting of the Committee of Management, 14th January, 1927, which established the "Dunning Fund"

COMMITTEE OF MANAGEMENT.

Minutes of Meeting held in the Victoria Law Courts, Birmingham, on Friday, 14th January, 1927.

Present: Sir Leonard Dunning.
Mr.B.D. Pinkerton (Chairman)
Messrs. E.E. Dalton
T.M. Harris
H.P. Hunter
F.H. Mardlin
C.C.H. Moriarty
F.W. Myers
T. Simpkins
W. Southwell
C.J.L. Hickling
J. Murray Laing, F.I.A., F.F.A.,
and the Secretary.

Letters of apology for absence were received from Mr. E. Holmes and Mr. R. Ross.

The Chairman referred to the loss which the Society had recently sustained in the death of Sir Robert Peacock. A letter of condolence had been despatched.

The Minutes of the last Meeting of the Committee of Management were read and approved on the proposal of Mr. Dalton, seconded by Mr. Moriarty.

The Chairman submitted correspondence since the last Committee Meeting re L.515 W.R. Cullen deceased. It was proposed by Mr. Southwell and seconded by Mr. Mardlin that the action taken by the Secretary be approved. Carried.

Sir Leonard Dunning informed the Meeting that he appealed in the Police Press for contributions to help an old pensioner and his wife, whose certificates (1.6253/4 Brinkman) had lapsed owing to the non-payment of premiums. Over £91 was received, from which amount £5 had been handed to Mr. Brinkman and £3.13.6 forwarded to the Secretary to liquidate the arrears owing at 27/12/26. Sir Leonard asked the Committee to relieve him of the balance of the sum collected, which he suggested should be applied to give assistance in any similar Whole Life cases which came to the notice of the Society.

tions, central heating, new electrical installations and cloakroom facilities. The total cost was just over £16,500.

At the 1960 Annual General Meeting in Scarborough, the Society noted, with regret, the death of Sir Frank Brook, its former President.

PMAS history was made at this meeting because it was the first time that details of the Society's investments were made available to delegates. The annual accounts were published in booklet form and so delegates and authorised officers were able to scrutinise the Society's investment portfolio.

The actuary, Kenneth Britt, explained, "The investments are well spread within the classes of securities available to the Society but you must remember that as a Registered Friendly Society (as the PMAS is) we are confined practically to trustee securities. A lot of thought is given to the Society's investments and they are reviewed from time to time."

Assets had risen to £3,884,000 by this time and the Society was obliged, by virtue of the National Insurance Act of 1959, to review its own pension scheme for employees. It was also reviewing its investment procedures and seeking wider powers of investment for its trustees; it also made application to become a member of Birmingham Chamber of Trade.

The pace of development was accelerating and there was a dramatic increase the following year (1961) following a massive pay award for police officers. The 1960 Royal Commission had learned that between the two World Wars, the pay and status of police officers was much higher than the average worker, but that since the end of World War II, the service had suffered a calamitous decline in both pay and status.

At first, police pay had not been included within the terms of reference of this Royal Commission and it was due to pressure

Minutes from Committee of Management meeting, 14th January, 1927 continued from the secretary of the Police Federation, PC Arthur Evans, that the Home Secretary reluctantly agreed to include police remuneration within the terms of reference. It was a master-stroke by the Federation. The Commission concluded that "police pay is at present inadequate either to inspire in the police and the community a sense of fair treatment or to attract to the service as a whole, and retain in it, enough recruits of the right standard."

The resultant pay increase was phenomenal by police standards; one account called it 'breathtaking'. The maximum pay for a constable rose from £695 per annum to £910 per annum and with two increments for long service, this rose to £970. It caused newspaper headlines to shout about "The £1,000 a year constable" and cartoonists to depict constables driving Rolls Royce cars. The constables' adjustments were followed with sergeants rising from £795 to £1,100, inspectors from £930 to £1,290 and chief inspectors from £1,050 to £1,445. Ranks above chief inspector were then faced with their own negotiations for pay increases, but the effect upon the PMAS was astonishing.

Police officers throughout the country decided to invest some of their new wealth in the PMAS and in the first four months of 1961, the Society transacted more business than in the whole of 1960.

The combined income of the PMAS (income from premiums at £810,000 and income from investments at £196,000) now exceeded £1,000,000 for the first time, while assets had passed the £4,000,000 mark and were rapidly soaring towards £5,000,000. It was a massive surge of income and wonderful show of confidence in the Society, yet it still managed to keep its management costs lower than 3% of premium income.

1961 was also marked by attendance at the Annual General Meeting by Mr A.H. Kennedy, the Inspector General of the Royal Ulster Constabulary, his first such visit to the PMAS. In his address to the delegates, Mr Kennedy reminded them that Mr Hadley had first visited the RUC in 1954 in what was described as a 'missionary role', since when members of that force had joined the PMAS. Now Mr Hadley and Mr King, his deputy, went twice a year to the RUC's depot at Enniskillen to talk with recruits where they convinced officers of the merits of the security offered by the PMAS.

That meeting was reminded of the provisions of the Trustee Investments Act of 1961 which would, when the Act was brought into force, permit investments in equity stocks. It would also give extended opportunities for investments which would benefit all members of the PMAS, even though fluctuations were bound to occur.

One consequence of that new legislation was that the PMAS established an Investment Sub-Committee to deal with its increasingly complex financial dealings.

There had, in fact, been a rapid increase in the volume of new business during the late 1950s, and this had produced a significant accumulation of funds for investment. Almost exclusively, these were channelled into fixed interest securities bearing in mind the restraints of the Trustee Act of 1925, albeit modified slightly by the Society's own rules.

The inaccessibility of equity-based growth opportunities was seriously jeopardising the Society's competitive potential to such an extent that earnest consideration had to be given (for probably the first, but certainly not the last time) to whether the future of the PMAS lay in transferring its status to that of a mutual company, thus achieving greater flexibility of operation (although subject to firm supervision by the then Board of Trade), or whether the prevailing serious investment restrictions were likely to be counter-balanced by tax exemptions and other advantages available under the less rigid and more friendly surveillance of the Chief Registrar of Friendly Societies.

Fortunately, that decision was avoided by the introduction of the Trustee Investments Bill, which, when it was enacted in 1961, afforded the PMAS wider powers of investment. These would include, *inter alia,* the ordinary stocks and shares of sizeable UK registered companies of proven profitable record. At the Annual Conference in Southport in May, 1961, a small meeting was held in a drab corner of the hotel lounge.

Its purpose, with some help from a visiting stockbroker, was to compile a list of companies whose shares would be monitored with a view to possible investment after implementation of the Act. That small group was the forerunner of the Society's Investment Sub-Committee.

It included the incumbents of the three non-executive professional posts most closely associated with the PMAS – the Consulting Actuary, the Manager of the New Street, Birmingham, branch of Lloyds Bank (the Society's bankers) and the senior partner of the firm of accountants appointed as approved auditor under the Friendly Societies Act. Over the years, men of distinction and acumen served in these capacities for varying lengths of time, and the Society was the continuing beneficiary of their skill and knowledge. The Investment Sub-Committee served in this form for some twenty five years, its end coming with the deregulation of the financial services industry.

Meanwhile another recurring theme presented itself. It was the question of allowing PMAS policies for children and for the possible creation of a Juvenile Section of the Society, but after much discussion, the proposal was again rejected.

In October 1961, the role of the Secretary of the PMAS came under scrutiny for it was appreciated that Mr Hadley was more of a manager than a secretary, and so his position was upgraded to "Manager & Secretary", a title which gave a more accurate description of his wide-ranging duties.

At this time, he announced that, surprisingly, only 40% of police officers were members of the PMAS. There was clearly a lot of work to be done, and he praised the RUC which already had 500 members from a strength of around 3,000; the London Metropolitan Police, on the other hand, had very few PMAS members because it still had its own Friendly Society and it was in the early months of 1962 that the Society received a request for admission by members of the Atomic Energy Authority Constabulary. This was rejected at that time, but its officers are now admitted to the Society.

The Society lost its auditor, Mr M.B. Hancock who had died tragically, and he was replaced by Mr C. J. Mason from the same accountants, Messrs Newton and Co. of Birmingham, and it was shortly afterwards that Mr Kenneth Britt announced his impending retirement. He had been involved with the PMAS long before his official appointment because it was he who had been approached in 1920 to provide the necessary advice to the founders. But because he had not then been a fully qualified actuary, the task was accepted by his chief, Mr Murray Laing.

Throughout Mr Murray Laing's work for the Society he was assisted by Mr Britt who had, in fact, helped to draw up the very first table of benefits for the PMAS Endowment Assurance Scheme table. He had also been closely connected with the work of transferring the old Police Mutual Assurance Association to the PMAS in 1921, more than 40 years ago. It was an impressive record of work for the PMAS. Illness prevented him speaking at the 1962 Annual General Meeting although he was present, and his report was read by Mr Hadley.

Mr Britt formally retired after presenting his December 1961 Quinquennial Report at that meeting. He was made an honorary Vice President and was succeeded by Mr N. A. Horsley, FIA, FFA, the deputy consulting actuary.

Before leaving, Mr Britt said that a summary of revenue accounts of the PMAS over a forty year period showed remarkable results which were without parallel in any other society or company founded during living memory. He continued by saying he had been proud to be associated with the Society, adding that his work with the PMAS had been one of the most rewarding tasks of his career. His Quinquennial Report said that new business during the last five years had far exceeded that of the previous five, and even that had been superseded by the record business of 1961 when 17,223 new policies were effected. He heartily congratulated the Committee of Management and all the staff on the very satisfactory position which had been disclosed.

Mr Britt's retirement marked the end of a very long, very happy and very beneficial relationship with the PMAS.

By the end of 1961, the Society's assets were more than £5,000,000 and expected to reach £6,000,000 before the end of 1962; premium income exceeded £1,000,000 and this phenomenal, rapidly expanding business produced praise from no less a figure than Sir Cecil Crabbe, the Chief Registrar of Friendly Societies. He added that the PMAS was always so outstanding that he always reported its progress to Parliament.

He described it as "spectacular" but such success did impose a great responsibility upon members of the Committee of Management and it was suggested that there was a change in the methods of investment, albeit within the rules laid down for friendly societies. Although the investment powers of trustees had been expanded, the PMAS still had only two funds – the Whole Life Fund and the Endowment Assurance Fund, and one suggestion was that the upper limit of the sum assured through the Endowment Fund be raised from £500 to £1,000. This was discussed at the meeting and Sir Cecil Crabbe explained the procedural problems in raising this amount, one of which was its firm link with the tax exemptions enjoyed by friendly societies. Because of tax concessions, the amount of £500 could not be increased – the Government had said 'No' and as Sir Cecil pointed out, the PMAS "would have to live with that 'no' for quite a long time."

By the beginning of 1963, it was possible for the amounts from maturing policies to be paid directly into officers' bank accounts, a move which has proved popular, but a new request was received. Married policewomen asked if their husbands could take out policies with the PMAS.

The question being asked was, "If the wife of a serving policeman is eligible, why can this not apply to the husband of a serving policewoman?" One argument against this was that it might include male civilians in hazardous occupations who were subjected to conditions which might impair health or shorten their lives. The matter was discussed at length by the Committee of Management in March 1963 but it was decided not to open the Endowment Scheme to the husbands of women police officers.

This coincided with a publicity campaign to recruit new members, the emphasis being placed upon the benefits of investing monies received through the 1961 pay increase. In addition, the Police Federation now agreed that PMAS posters could be displayed at their annual conferences. The first such occasion would be at Blackpool in 1963 and they assured the Society that its advertising material would be welcomed at all future Police Federation conferences and meetings. This would complement the popular PMAS calendars and *Police Review* diaries some of which now bore special PMAS covers.

At the 1963 Annual General Meeting in Llandudno, the vice chairman of the town council produced the slogan, "Look after the coppers and the pounds will look after themselves", but a sombre note was introduced by the announcement of the death of Mr Kenneth Britt, the recently retired actuary.

Delegates stood in silent tribute and it was then announced that the Society's President, Sir William Johnson (who was in fact Her Majesty's first Chief Inspector of Constabulary), wished to formally retire from the presidency. This was noted with regret, and he was succeeded by Mr E.J. (later Sir Edward) Dodd, CBE, a Vice President and then Chief Constable of Birmingham, who was to follow Sir William as HM Chief Inspector of Constabulary.

At this meeting, the Society announced reaching the target of £6,000,000 worth of assets and now expanded its operations by accepting premiums from the Jersey Paid Police on condition that

Sir Edward Dodd

the force appointed an authorised officer and arranged for deductions for premiums to be made from pay. A more important innovation was also announced at this time. It was the implementation of the Society's own long-awaited house purchase scheme. Agreement had been reached between the Woolwich Equitable Building Society and the PMAS to jointly launch a scheme which would be beneficial to police officers who wished to purchase their own houses. There was a growing desire among serving officers to become property owners, even among those stationed in county forces, and the scheme was met with wide approval.

A publicity campaign was immediately launched and with this plan, the PMAS embarked on the first of several new financial schemes for the benefit of police officers.

Another new idea was to give a prize for the best student of every initial training course at each of the country's police training centres. It was proposed that the PMAS should donate a book token to the value of two guineas (£2. 2s. 0d – £2.10) for each winning student and, with some minor modification, this was to become known as the PMAS Book Prize. Commandants of the various training centres were then approached for their approval, and it seems that all welcomed this initiative.

The first awards were at the Scottish Police College (junior division) and the Royal Ulster Constabulary depot at Enniskillen. Training centres in England and Wales were later to adopt the prize and by 1965 the Book Prize was in full operation throughout Great Britain. The prize was a dictionary which was awarded to the recruit showing the highest academic merit in three examinations during the initial training course.

Further acts of benevolence were implemented by gifts of £1,000 to the Police Convalescent Homes at Hove and Harrogate. By the autumn of that year (1963), it was clear that even the extended premises at No. 10 Greenfield Crescent were becoming too cramped for the expanding Society, and approval was sought for another extension.

There were some rather unsightly outhouses which could be demolished to make way for an extension and these changes were approved.

Before they could be implemented, however, Head Office suffered an embarrassment – the offices were broken into, with some petty cash being stolen and some furnishings damaged. This prompted the Society to install burglar alarms although its important papers were already in either fire proof cabinets or secure storage at Lloyds Bank in Birmingham.

Acceptance of the Society's House Purchase Scheme led to the Woolwich Equitable Building Society being invited to the next annual general meeting. This was at Bangor in 1964, the first time the PMAS had met in Northern Ireland. It was also the first such address by an officer of the Woolwich, but it was the forerunner of many. In this case, the Assistant General Manager of the Woolwich congratulated the PMAS on its annual figures and then explained how the jointly operated house purchase scheme would function, saying that he looked forward to the time, in the fairly near future, when members would be receiving mortgage advances of between £1,000,000 and £2,000,000 per year. By this stage, the PMAS assets had reached £7,000,000 even though it was still limited in the scope and size of the policies it could offer. The Society noted that the police had been awarded another substantial pay rise with effect from September 1964, which prompted a further surge in advertising and publicity, but once again, the possibility of a scheme for police pensioners was rejected.

Nonetheless, a new idea did enter the discussion – this was a proposal that police cadets should be allowed to join the PMAS. The Committee of Management decided to examine this latest suggestion with their usual care.

Early in 1965, the staff at Head Office became excited because there was a possibility that the semi-detached house adjoining their premises, No. 11 Greenfield Crescent, Edgbaston, would be for sale. If this was true, and if the Society could purchase No. 11, the ever-present problem of lack of space at No. 10 might be solved for some considerable time ahead. The Standing Sub-Committee was authorised to examine this possibility.

Later, it was reported that No. 11 had been valued at £18,500 and the PMAS decided to make an offer to buy the premises. Sadly, the offer for sale was later withdrawn, and it was evident that, very soon, the PMAS would have to consider yet further extensions to No. 10 Greenfield Crescent, or alternatively seek new offices. Any possible extension of No. 10 was very restricted and it was decided that the only solution lay in a brand new custom-built office block and so began the long hunt for a site. At this time, however, the Labour Government had imposed restrictions on the building of new offices and so an extension of the existing building appeared to be the only viable solution, however limiting that might be.

It was in May 1965, that the PMAS made application to join the National Conference of Friendly Societies, a body which represented the leading 100 friendly societies in Britain. The benefits were that the National Conference existed to protect the interests of friendly societies and their members; it watched over proceedings in Parliament which affected societies and their members and took action on their behalf when necessary; it furthered and defended the interests and privileges of the societies and it took any action which was necessary or desirable to promote improvements in the Friendly Societies Acts. After due discussion, it was decided that the PMAS should apply for membership so that it could play its part in the work of the National Conference.

When the PMAS held its 38th Annual General Meeting in Dunblane, Perthshire in May 1965, it was attended by what was described as the most formidable array of chief constables ever to grace its annual meeting, and among them were twenty chief constables from Scotland. Also present was Mr J.A.R. Murray, the ex-Chief Constable of Motherwell and Wishaw who had been an authorised officer of the PMAS for over 30 years.

Cordial welcomes were extended to Mr T. Renfrew, CBE, HM Chief Inspector of Constabulary for Scotland, Mr A. Meldrum, OBE, the HMI for Scotland and Miss Janet Gray, BEM, the Assistant HMI for Scotland. Mr Renfrew told the meeting how he had joined the PMAS.

As a very new constable on parade, the authorised officer said, "You are all in the PMAS and that'll mean a bob a week off your pay!" But, as Mr Renfrew said, "When that 'bob' had matured with interest, it paid a very satisfactory sum. I wish I'd been put in for three bob!" But it was a typical police method of finding volunteers!

The meeting heard yet more stories of the phenomenal success of the PMAS, with assets rising to over £8,587,000 and the number of new policies, the aftermath of the recent pay increase, averaging 46 for every working day of the year, or an average of almost 1,000 a month, a further tribute to the hard work of the authorised officers.

During 1965, the house purchase scheme was getting under way very satisfactorily with over £1,000,000 being advanced to PMAS members for mortgages by the Woolwich Equitable Building Society in the year ended September 1965, but earlier that year, PMAS assets had shown depreciation because the Labour Government had increased the bank rate from 4% to 7%, as a result of which the Stock Exchange had been producing much reduced figures and wide fluctuations following a most involved Budget. Even so, the PMAS would continue to show a good return on its investments for its members.

At the 1965 AGM, the acceptance of police cadets as PMAS members was approved and it was also agreed that cash surrender values on Endowment policies could be paid after only six months duration of the policies.

By October that year, some 230 policies had been issued to cadets, but some forces were not allowing their premiums to be deducted from pay. The Society agreed to try to persuade them to adopt that procedure although the cadets who were members would not be pressurised into adopting this. There were some minor problems with members of the Whole Life Section; since all their policies had been made paid-up in 1957, some of them had not kept the Society informed of their circumstances or changes in address. Indeed, some had died without their relatives notifying Head Office and so a large-scale attempt was made to trace 'missing' members and their beneficiaries.

One suggestion was that, because of the advanced age of surviving members, it might be possible to change the rules so that their policies produced a cash settlement before death. Some pensioners were in dire financial straits and this would ease their burden. The proposal was approved at the 1966 AGM, a nice gesture for those who wished to make use of it.

Towards the end of 1965, the PMAS launched an advertising campaign in the national press and at the same time, sought authority, through the Friendly Societies Liaison Committee, to increase the £500 limit of its sums assured. For endowment assurance policies, that limit was imposed on all friendly societies but within the year, the limit was raised to a maximum of £2,500 per person, albeit with only the first £500 being allowed for tax exemption but it meant that the PMAS could now expand its range of policies.

The 1966 AGM at Cambridge was unusual because the Society was welcomed to the city by a former police officer. It was the first time the Society had received a civic welcome from a former police officer; he was Alderman H.G. Ives, the Mayor of Cambridge, and a former member of Cambridge City Police. It was announced at this meeting that gross income had now exceeded £2,000,000 per annum, with income from premiums being the highest on record at £1,602,000, while at the date of the meeting, assets had passed the £10,000,000 level. The house purchase scheme was flourishing and the Committee of Management was now faced with modernising the Society's accounting system.

It was in need of a complete overhaul because the existing system for the old machinery was unable to cope with the increasing demands. Mechanisation of the systems dealing with the accounts and with new business was urgently required, and so approval for a programme of modernisation was sought and approved.

In October 1966, however, it was noted that approval had been granted for an additional floor to the existing extension at No. 10 Greenfield Crescent, but would this latest increase in space be sufficient for the inevitable future expansion of the PMAS? John Hadley feared not. He realised that the only viable solution was a completely new building and announced that a search for a site was already being made.

Under consideration were sites in Birmingham, Bournville, Droitwich, Coventry and Redditch while another option was to consider sites in the New Development Areas of Great Britain. These included various parts of the North of England, Wales, the West Country and Scotland. The Board of Trade would offer help in finding a site in one of the New Development Areas and would also offer a grant of 25% of the building cost, but in spite of the attractiveness of such a grant, none of the areas was suitable and some presented complications. The Board of Trade did point out, however, that it could not offer a permit for an office in the Midlands as that was not a New Development Area and also because PMAS business was not restricted to the Midlands – it could be conducted anywhere in the British Isles.

Of all the options, and bearing in mind the nature of PMAS business and its links with every UK police force, Droitwich emerged as the favourite site and the town's local government officials began to court the PMAS, saying they'd like the Society to become a part of the town's central development. In April 1967, the PMAS made an offer to negotiate for the first office block to be built in the Droitwich Town Centre Development Plan; the offer allowed monies for construction of a new office block with a reserve for future investment, but differences between Droitwich Rural District Council and Worcestershire County Council were to delay the proposed Town Development Plan.

The PMAS could only wait – and continue its frustrating search for another suitable site in case this proposal did not materialise. It was vital that the PMAS did find a suitable site because its work was rapidly expanding and new members of staff were necessary. There was a desperate shortage of office space in No. 10 Greenfield Crescent and permission was sought to install a temporary portable building in the garden. This would suffice for perhaps a further two years, but it was necessary because the Secretary reported that there was a need for the Society to expand its range of assurance cover. The proposals included:

    (a)   short term endowment assurance (5–9 years);

    (b)   whole life cover;

    (c)   annuities;

    (d)   mortgage protection policies.

It was also necessary to improve the Society's existing practice of granting loans on the security of policies. The need to expand the PMAS range of cover resulted from competition by other commercial organisations, including insurance companies, unit trusts and savings schemes but, until now, the PMAS, as a friendly society, had been restricted in the range of policies it could offer. The Society's new Consulting Actuary, Mr K. Muir McKelvey, who had stepped in at short notice due to the illness, prior to retirement, of the former actuary, Mr N.A. Horsley, said that many officers were investing with other commercial life assurance companies.

He suggested that the modest limit of £500 endowment assurance per member might be one reason. Even with bonuses added, £500 had not been an attractively large sum to receive upon maturity after a long period of saving; other assurance companies, who were not restricted by the rules governing friendly societies, were able to offer higher sums upon maturity and many police officers were investing with them instead of the PMAS.

As the benefits offered by various commercial schemes were examined, the Society's advisers discovered a somewhat unexpected competitor – the Police Federation. It was about to announce its own Death Benefit Group Insurance Scheme and when the PMAS informed the Federation that its scheme conflicted with forthcoming PMAS plans, the Federation replied that it could not withdraw its plans as they were too advanced.

The PMAS, who regarded the Federation as a friend and ally, had therefore to devise some attractive and competitive new schemes if it was to expand its service to police officers. The go-ahead was given when the Government lifted the £500 endowment limit on friendly society members; that change provided the opportunity for major expansion.

The outcome was that in 1967 the PMAS did broaden its range with endowment policies offering a limit of £2,500 per member as opposed to £500; this was increased to £3,500 when used as mortgage protection for house purchase.

There was the extremely popular 'Panda' scheme which gave very high death cover for a very low premium, with an added endowment content, and there were also short-term policies of between five and nine years duration. The loan scheme was improved and these innovations had the desired affect because new business transacted during 1967 broke all previous records – over 18,900 policies were issued for sums assured in excess of £12,600,000.

Extract from 1931 PMAS diary

List of County, City and Borough Police Forces in England, Wales and Scotland, with the Names of Chief Constables, Authorised Strength of each Force, Membership of the P.M.A.S. at 30/6/30, and Authorised Officers of the Society.

ENGLAND.

County Force.	Chief Constable.	Strength.	Member-ship.	Authorised Officer.
Bedfordshire	Lt.-Col. F. A. D. Stevens, C.B.E., D.L.	142	75	P.C. K. Simpson, Leighton Buzzard.
Berkshire	Lt.-Col. A. F. Poulton, C.B.E.	267	12	Supt. A. W. Sellwood, Reading.
Buckinghamshire	Col. T. R. P. Warren, C.B.E.	239	47	P.C. E. Randall, Little Brickhill, Bletchley.
	W. V. Webb	73	92	Supt. A. E. Allen, Cambridge.
Cambridgeshire	Lt.-Col. P. Malcolm, D.S.O., M.V.O.	558	2	P.C. L. P. Blewett, Bodmin.
Cheshire	Lt.-Col. Sir H. B. Protheroe- Smith, O.B.E.	271	40	Insp. R. S. Dickinson, Penrith.
	T. B. Browne	285	75	Supt. W. Wood, Ashbourne.
	...ley, C.B.E.	444	103	Supt. H. H. Champion, Crown Hill.
		424	198	

It was in 1967 that a new President was announced – he was Sir Eric St. Johnston, CBE, HM Chief Inspector of Constabulary and he succeeded Sir Edward Dodd who had died the previous September after long and valuable service as the President of the PMAS. But one anniversary was almost overlooked. 1967 was in fact the centenary of the PMAS – there had been 55 years of the old Police Mutual Assurance Association followed immediately by 45 years of the present Police Mutual Assurance Society. A modest note of this anniversary was mentioned by Mr E.S. Drake, Chairman of the Management Committee, in his speech to the Annual Conference that year.

It was in September 1967 that two new members of the Head Office staff were appointed – one was Mr Philip R. Woollard, ACII and the other was Mr Peter J. Sharpe, ACII. Both were appointed Assistant Secretaries. Mr Woollard was a keen Round Tabler while Mr Sharpe was a sportsman who played hockey for the Midlands as well as being a minor county cricketer.

Mr. J. Wright, Chairman, and Mr. J. W. Hadley, Manager & Secretary, inspecting a flexo-writer machine which produced punched tapes which in turn helped to produce new policy and related documents

They arrived at a time of great change within the Society but also as another massive change was looming in the fairly near future. It was one which would stretch their administrative capabilities, for it was the impending decimalisation of the British currency. This would involve a massive amount of additional work, not least of which was the conversion of all the policies from £.s.d. to decimal currency. But, as Mr Hadley said of these young men less than six months after their appointment, "They have settled in extremely well and have already proved their worth during a hectic and busy period of expansion."

But they were to be faced with an even more challenging and exciting future because, after a long and very difficult search, a site for a new office block had been found. It had previously borne an old gasworks and looked anything but appealing but it was two acres in extent, the freehold had been offered and the price was most reasonable.

The Board of Trade had agreed to an Office Building Permit, outline planning permission had been granted and detailed plans were being prepared. The site was in Queen Street at Lichfield and even as these plans were being made, the delighted staff of the PMAS, who had endured less than perfect office accommodation for many years, were talking of moving in the spring of 1970 and of holding the 1970 annual conference, with due pomp and ceremony, in their splendid new building.

1967 closed as the annual income reached £2,573,911, an all-time record. It was yet another outstanding year for the PMAS with the possibility of still more exciting times ahead.

Illustration from Ladybird Book, originals from which hang in the boardroom at Alexandra House.

119

SELECTED CONTRIBUTIONS

In assembling information for inclusion in this book, we approached many people who were, or who had been, associated with the PMAS over the years. Most of their memories and reminiscences are included within the text but it was felt that some contributions were worthy of reproduction in their entirety.

One came from Alan King, OBE, FCII, who was Manager & Secretary of the PMAS from 1975 until 1986. Here he reminisces upon the then new Head Office and the first meeting of the Committee of Management following his appointment as Assistant Secretary in 1954.

"Situated in the up-market area of Edgbaston, the new office's location was to prove an inspired choice because not only did many other business houses subsequently follow to the area, but the prestigious Birmingham Chamber of Industry and Commerce decided to vacate its city centre headquarters in favour of a larger, purpose-built office block a mere few yards around the corner from the Society's new home. Thus by happy chance, or, more fairly, by the prescience of John Hadley and Jim Wright in judging the future pattern of office development, the PMAS found itself operating from the very kernel of Midlands business life.

Not only was the Society to become a member of the Chamber and to widen its circle of important business contacts and influence (also, through its membership, to be associated with the Chamber's great joint project with the City of Birmingham, the National Exhibition Centre), but it also made full use of its comprehensive modern facilities for Committee and Sub-Committee meetings and other functions. Throughout the remainder of the Society's domicile in Edgbaston – some 15 years – the Chamber was to prove an ideal adjunct to our pleasing, albeit latterly cramped, but homely office.

The first Committee of Management meeting of the new regime was held within a few weeks of our taking office and the venue was the Grand Jury Room of the Victoria Law Courts, a few steps down the road from our then Headquarters. It was a memorable experience.

The Chairman, Chief Inspector Stan Drake of the City of Birmingham Police, whom I had already met thanks to a typical gesture of this kindly gentleman in having called in with a word of welcome on my first day, gave an expert demonstration of a no-nonsense approach to the conduct of a meeting. No one was denied his contribution to the discussions, but any diversion from the business in hand, from whomsoever, top brass or otherwise, was quickly and firmly suppressed.

And what personalities they were: Mr W.C. Johnson, an Inspector of Constabulary and former Chief Constable of Birmingham (later to become Sir William, Her Majesty's first Chief Inspector of Constabulary, and President of the Society); Mr E. J. Dodd, the then incumbent Chief Constable of Birmingham (himself later to become Chief Inspector of Constabulary, President of the Society and knighted as Sir Edward); Sir Herbert Hunter, Inspector A.E. Treves; Chief Inspector Alfred Wyles, Birmingham's Summons and Warrants Officer who was, over the years, to prove a doughty opponent to any significant progress being made, or so it seemed, particularly if it involved the expenditure of money. Alf Wyles was by nature a rebel, despite his professional status as a paragon of the establishment, and he thrived on controversial debate. His contribution should not be dismissed as unhelpful, however, for he taught us the discipline of ensuring that no case, no matter how innocuous or trivial, should ever be put before the Committee without it having been thoroughly prepared. It was a lesson to be learned well and one which was to be of immeasurable value in later life."

CHAPTER 4

INTO THE COMPUTER ERA

1968 – 1986

As the PMAS entered the final years of the 1960s, there was much to occupy its staff and Committee of Management. For one thing, there was the pressure of planning and erecting their new Head Office in its two phases. The first was intended to be the construction of an office block with car park and caretaker's house, and second would be other accommodation, possibly domestic. In addition, there was the impending decimalisation of the nation's currency. This would require a tremendous effort by the staff in converting thousands of policies, making new calculations, drawing up new tables of benefit and re-designing forms of application. To add to the pressure, there was also the first of two series of police force amalgamations which would add to the administrative difficulties faced by an already very busy staff. Those amalgamations would reduce the number of forces from 126 to only 47. Officers would find themselves serving in forces bearing names which were different from the ones they had joined, and their forces would have different boundaries which would require detailed amendments to Head Office files. Furthermore, authorised officers would have to cope with changed county, city and borough treasurers who used different procedures for making premium deductions from pay.

At that time, few offices boasted computerised records and so most of this enormous task had to be undertaken in the old fashioned way – by hand. Both authorised officers and head office staff had long experience of the chore of record keeping by hand, especially at month-end when ledgers had to be balanced. Almost everyone involved with the PMAS began to appreciate that new technology must soon take over some of those routine tasks. It was just a matter of time before the old practices were regarded as obsolete.

But the PMAS does not waste time bemoaning its problems – without delay, it gets down to solving them and, in the early months of 1968, it even made time to formulate a new loan scheme by which members could borrow up to 90% of the surrender value of their endowment policies. This could be done either as a temporary loan over one or two years with monthly repayments, or on a permanent basis with interest only payable in arrears. This excited a great deal of interest, particularly at a time when borrowing from banks had been restricted by the Labour Government then in power, and the scheme won warm praise from a grateful membership.

Another well supported scheme was the famous 'Panda' policy which had been introduced during 1967 but was already proving such a success. This was designed to meet the need for high death cover at very low cost and it was to prove a long-running favourite, one utilised by a high proportion of the membership.

During the early months, however, the PMAS was to suffer the loss of one of its major personalities, the splendid Captain Wood who had been such a fine and efficient secretary. He died on 2nd March 1968, having been Secretary to the Society from 1922 until 1954. But even as his death was being mourned, a new stalwart was making his presence felt.

He was a man called John Furber, a Chief Superintendent in the Cheshire force who had been appointed to the Committee of Management. He was welcomed to his first meeting in March 1968 when it was hoped it would be a long and cordial relationship. Those words were prophetic indeed for Mr Furber has been with the PMAS ever since and at the time of writing is Chairman of the Committee of Management, one of only five holders of that office since the formation of the Society. The words 'long' and 'cordial' perfectly describe his association with the PMAS.

As plans for the new Head Office intensified, a Building Sub-Committee, chaired by Mr J. Wright, MBE, the former Deputy Chief Constable of Staffordshire and including Mr E.S. Drake, the Society's Chairman, and Mr J.F. Lumley, was appointed to oversee every aspect of its construction in conjunction with Mr John Hadley, Manager & Secretary. Meanwhile the work of the Society continued at Edgbaston. Then in May 1968, a strip of land adjoining the new site came on the market. It was a small piece, only some 648 square yards in area, but the asking price was £1,600 and it did adjoin the western boundary of the new Head Office site.

It was an opportunity that could not be ignored and so the land was bought, thus increasing the assets of the PMAS.

By the end of 1967, the total assets had risen to £12 million which signified yet another year of unprecedented progress. In 1968, Mr Wright had been elected to another post, that of Deputy Chairman of the Committee of Management, and the Society was making its presence known in other areas.

The Deputy Manager & Secretary, Alan King, attended the Annual Conference of the National Conference of Friendly Societies at Eastbourne in September while it was decided to augment the visits to District Police Training Centres by calling on Force Authorised Officers.

The first visit to an Authorised Officer was at Winchester in Hampshire and it proved a most beneficial innovation. It highlighted some of the problems which had arisen due to both the increasing complexity of life insurance and the 1968 amalgamation of police forces. The former was raising some very technical questions in the minds of potential members, questions that required an expert response, while the latter led to larger force areas with larger divisions containing a greater number of officers. It became clear that the Force Authorised Officers needed some help – so the PMAS produced a manual for their use but in recognition

MR JAMES WRIGHT,
MBE, O ST J, QPM

Jim Wright joined the Staffordshire Police Force in 1925 and became a Sergeant in 1934, followed by promotion to Inspector in 1939 and Superintendent in 1940. By the end of the war, he had been promoted to Chief Superintendent and rose to become second Assistant Chief Constable in 1958, a post he held until taking over as Deputy Chief Constable in 1961. Upon the amalgamation of the Staffordshire and Stoke City Forces, he became Assistant Chief Constable of the new force until his retirement in March, 1968 after 42 years in the service.

Mr Wright became a member of the Society in the early days of his career and served as a successful Authorised Officer for many years, both before and after the war, when he took on appointments of greater responsibility in the Society's affairs. Elected to the General Committee in 1946, Mr Wright joined the Accounts Sub-Committee in 1949. In 1963, he was elected a Vice President and in 1969, became Chairman, a post he was to hold for eleven years.

Mr Wright was devoted to the Society and his contribution to its development and to staff pay and conditions was immense. As Chairman of the Building Committee in the late 1960s, he was largely responsible for moving the Society into its present fine Head Office at Alexandra House in Lichfield.

In 1973, he was elected to Life Vice President, an honour he deeply valued.

of the fact that the Society needed wider representation within police forces, it also sought to establish divisional representatives throughout the country.

They would not assume the role of Authorised Officers, but would be there to assist in the distribution of literature, posters and promotional material, to answer simple questions and generally to ease the burden of the Authorised Officer. The innovations were welcomed and these, plus a pay rise for the police, did result in a welcome boost of new business.

The continuing success of the PMAS and its highly special-ised role as the police officers' own assurance society, continued to attract the interest of police forces other than those of our counties and cities. This was a regular occurrence and the Society even attracted requests for membership from overseas.

In 1969, the British Transport Police made a formal approach for its officers to be allowed membership of the PMAS and the Society responded by saying that one of its conditions was that its members must allow their premiums to be deducted at source from their pay. BTP replied by saying its members wanted to make use of the Post Office Giro System, but refused to allow deduc-tions from its officers' pay – and so its request for membership was declined. The facility of deducting premiums at source from officers' pay was to become an important condition when other specialised or smaller police forces later began to apply for mem-bership of the PMAS.

During 1969, work commenced on the new Head Office, the contractors being F. and E.V. Linford of Cannock in Stafford-shire.

Very soon, the steel frame of the building took shape. Even as this work was in progress, however, the cramped offices at No. 10, Greenfield Crescent in Edgbaston were proving far too small, even for just another few months. Fortunately, there was an opportu-nity for the Society to temporarily rent a room almost opposite, at No. 7, Greenfield Crescent, and this offer was accepted. Thus the offices of the PMAS straddled the road in Greenfield Crescent, but the extra space provided a most welcome, if short term, respite as the staff looked forward to the completion of the new building.

But would it be ready for the 1970 Annual Conference? That was the question uppermost in the minds of many, for it had already been suggested that Lichfield might be the host city and that the meetings might take place within the fine new offices. The contractor had promised a completion date of 16th January 1970, and if this was met, then the AGM, always held in May or June, could make use of the new facilities, even allowing for a short delay.

It was in May 1969 that the Society learned it was to lose one of its chairmen of the Committee of Management. He was Mr E.S. Drake, such a stalwart supporter who announced his impending retirement. He had served on the committee since 1932, a period of 37 years, and had been Chairman since 1952. He was appointed a Life Vice President in recognition of his services.

It was later to emerge that Mr Drake's father, himself a police officer, had been an authorised officer in the early days of the old Police Mutual Assurance Association and had appointed the young Drake as a collector of premiums. Thus the family association with the PMAA and the PMAS extended over a very long period. Mr. J. Wright was elected Chairman of the Management Committee to succeed Mr. Drake, with Mr. J.F. Lumley as his deputy.

As the Society's assets soared to £14 million, there was rising concern about the delays to the construction of the new Head Office. One minor problem was a right of way which ran through the land but this was not causing building delays; these were due to difficulties in obtaining the correct windows and the result was that, by September 1969, work was some seven weeks behind schedule. This news came at a time when plans were well advanced for the 1970 conference to be held there, with the additional bonus that this might incorporate the official opening ceremony which was to be conducted by a member of the Royal family. But when detailed enquiries were made among Lichfield's hotels, it was discovered they were inadequate for the projected conference – it could not, after all, be held at the new Head Office and so, rather belatedly, it was re-scheduled to take place in June at the Crown Hotel in Scarborough. The official opening of Head Office would be a separate occasion, probably in April or May of 1970. But there was further bad news – just as plans were being re-arranged, the Crown Hotel announced that it was being sold and so another bout of last-minute arrangements had to be made.

Fortunately, the St Nicholas Hotel in Scarborough, last visited in 1951 by the PMAS Annual Conference, had been extended and modernised and it was able to accommodate the conference. At last, the conference arrangements could be completed, but news of building progress was awaited because plans for its Royal opening ceremony had to be finalised and there was also the question of the timing of the disposal of No. 10, Greenfield Crescent in Edgbaston.

Meanwhile, the Society had invested in a small computer, the forerunner of an eventual major investment in new technology. This early machine was a miniature computer which proved ideal for calculating surrender values of policies but it is probably fair to say that it heralded a major shift of emphasis because it was a small step in the recognition of a need for new technology, particularly as the legal and practical aspects of life insurance were rapidly changing and becoming infinitely more complex. The Labour Government had imposed its Selective Employment Tax which added substantially to the costs of employing staff while the Family Law Reform Act of 1969 had reduced the age of majority from 21 to 18, thus affecting some friendly societies who would not allow persons under 21 to sit upon committees. This did not affect the PMAS.

As the 1960s drew to a close, the builders of Head Office produced some splendid work to overcome the earlier delay and the Society was able, with confidence, to plan its transfer from

Edgbaston to Queen Street in Lichfield.

It was scheduled to take place over the weekend of 14th and 15th February 1970. The entire office contents would be moved so that work could continue as normal from 9am on Monday 16th February 1970. A caretaker had been appointed for the new building and HRH The Princess Alexandra had graciously consented to perform the official opening ceremony. That was planned for 24th March 1970 and the building would be named in her honour – Alexandra House. And No. 10 Greenfield Crescent, Edgbaston was put on the market.

A view of the newly completed Alexandra House 1970

By the date of the removal to Alexandra House, the building work was complete, apart from some landscaping of the grounds, and it was agreed by all that the standard of workmanship was superb and the design was excellent. In short, all members of staff were delighted with their new working conditions and many sold their houses to live closer to their new place of employment. Immediately, however, they busied themselves with plans for the opening ceremony; there was a great deal to consider such as the catering, guest list, police arrangements, choice of marquee, tables, chairs, cutlery, table linen, car parking, lighting, heating, the itinerary....it was an exciting time but all this hard work was rewarded by a charming Princess Alexandra. She showed a deep interest in the staff and in the work of the Society as she met them afterwards and toured the building.

However, in the midst of all the happiness, the work of the Society had to continue without interruption.

Sadly, Mr P. R. Woollard, the Assistant Secretary, resigned in June 1970 after making a great contribution to the work of the PMAS; he wished to further his career elsewhere and left with deep regret; he was replaced by Mr P. H. Crawford, ACII. As these changes were being undertaken, the Society was considering the introduction of a new type of insurance.

It was an endowment scheme linked to a unit trust and it would be known as The Unit Trust Endowment Scheme. It was pointed out that the Society's conventional endowment scheme was, in fact, two policies within a single contract. One provided a term of assurance with a cash payment on death and the other produced an endowment with a cash payment upon maturity after an agreed term of years. With this system, a policyholder could never lose, and with the success of the PMAS investment policy, such policies would produce a handsome return. But the new policy, which was tied to Lloyds Bank Second Unit Trust, allowed the policyholder to take a risk because his premiums would be invested in an approved unit trust. If the unit trust investments

Scenes from the formal opening of Alexandra House by HRH Princess Alexandra

Top left HRH Princess Alexandra speaking to PC John Stephen, Drum Major of the City of Birmingham Police Pipe Band

Top right Authorised Officers meet Princess Alexandra. They are (from left to right), PC A. C. R. Hounsell (Metropolitan Police), Chief Inspector J. F. Jones (Thames Valley), Sergeant E. G. C. Ireland (Suffolk), Chief Superintendent F. Cowcill (West Midlands) and PC J. B. Clarke (Nottinghamshire)

Centre HRH Princess Alexandra, accompanied by the Lord Lieutenant of Staffordshire, is welcomed to Alexandra House. (From left to right) Mr. A. F. King (Deputy Manager), Mr. J. W. Hadley (Manager & Secretary), Mr. J. Wright (Chairman), Sir Eric St. Johnston (President) shaking hands with HRH, Bishop G. E. Holderness (Dean of Lichfield), Dr. A. S. Reeve (Bishop of Lichfield)

Bottom Soldiers of the band of the Junior Soldiers Company, Whittington Barracks, outside Alexandra House

performed well, then the policyholder would benefit; if the unit trust lost money, then the policyholder might not gain such generous benefits although in such cases, the insurers would guarantee a minimum return.

Either way, the policyholder would gain and this new policy was seen as one for the more mature officer with a little extra cash to invest and just a hint of risk attached. The sum guaranteed over a ten year period was £500, and over 15 years it rose to £750, with a minimum premium of just £1 per week. Instead of taking cash upon maturity, the policyholder could choose trust units which could be either retained or cashed at a later date. This scheme was approved by the Committee of Management on 16th June 1970 and so expanded the range of policies on offer. It was a major step when compared with the early days of the Society when only one type of policy was available.

With younger officers in mind, the Society also began to target new recruits by publishing two leaflets aimed at younger officers – one was called 'Getting Married' and the other was 'New Arrival', each proffering specialist insurance advice for officers facing those domestic changes. Another idea for younger officers was COP, the Convertible Option Policy, see page 137.

But it was then the turn of the pensioners. They began to demand special treatment by the PMAS. One of the recurring questions asked of the PMAS was why retired police officers could not become members.

Perhaps some of them did not understand that as a person grows older, the chance of death increases and such a person is therefore a greater risk to an insurer. On purely commercial terms, a retired officer did present a high, or even an unacceptable, risk to any life assurance company – but individual officers were not thinking in wider terms. They were thinking of themselves and so it was, after much consideration, that the Committee of Management agreed to permit retired officers to become members of the PMAS, but only if they had retired upon ordinary pension and only if they wished to replace contracts which were approaching maturity. An officer who had retired on pension, having never been a member, could not join the PMAS after the date of retirement. But it was possible to join before retirement and then replace the matured contract at a later date. This was a breakthrough for pensioners and whilst it did not placate every one of them, it did do something towards their overall welfare. This change, deeply discussed during 1970, was implemented early in 1971.

Head Office continued its move towards acceptance of new technology by investing in an NCR Accounting Machine and later a Farrington 1010 data processor, and it was able to extend its hospitality by inviting the National Conference of Friendly Societies to hold its quarterly meeting in the Alexandra House boardroom. This was accepted and the meeting occurred in July 1970 to enhance the reputation of the PMAS among its peers.

It was around this time that the Society decided to review its entire advertising policy. There was concern that, in spite of its earnest endeavours, there were still many police officers who were not members, some of them accepting the terms of commercial companies rather than those of their own Society. Some force magazines, for example, were not produced by the forces themselves, but published by advertising agencies who sold space for their own benefit; similar systems were used to publish diaries, sporting programmes and annual reports on athletic association

PRESIDENT

Sir Eric St. Johnston

PRESIDENT ELECT

John A. McKay

PROFESSIONAL ADVISERS

C. J. Mason
Auditor

K. M. McKelvey
Actuary

J. J. Thomas
Hon. Treasurer

VICE-PRESIDENTS

Sir Arthur Young

Sir Derrick Capper

Sir William Williams

EXECUTIVE OFFICERS

J. W. Hadley

A. F. King

David Gray

A. M. Rees

James Wright

P. J. Sharpe

P. H. Crawford

COMMITTEE OF MANAGEMENT

W. Baharie

J. G. Bentley

J. F. Lumley

P. Simpson

F. A. Smith

LIFE VICE-PRESIDENT

J. R. Furber

R. H. Jones

A. E. Treves

T. W. Whitefoot

E. S. Drake

Committee of Management and officers 1970

activities. The PMAS therefore decided not to advertise in such periodicals, but it would continue to support force magazines and similar publications which were produced solely by police forces.

In spite of the Society's advertising campaigns, it continued to rely heavily upon the services of its authorised officers, but it was acutely aware that the 1968 amalgamation programme had changed the face of the police service. Larger units with fewer authorised officers had been created.

Thus there was a reduced PMAS representation among serving officers and indeed, there was also committee representation in fewer forces. It was considered vital that the PMAS be well represented among the serving officers. One drawback was that, although the Society had urged forces to recruit divisional representatives, not every force had complied with this request.

Out of the 47 forces in England and Wales, only 25 had divisional representatives; out of the 20 forces in Scotland, only 4 had divisional representatives. There was still a need for further co-operation from chief constables with emphasis upon a wider representation within forces, and the Society would work towards that goal. One desire was to see at least one representative from every force at the Annual General Meeting; preferably it should be the Authorised Officer.

In the months which followed, a new development occurred. Police forces began to arrange their own PMAS conferences comprising the authorised officers and divisional representatives, and members of Head Office staff began to receive invitations to address these meetings. It was a welcome innovation, and it was supplemented by a standing invitation from Head Office for authorised officers, divisional representatives and indeed any officer, to visit Alexandra House and enjoy its facilities. This coincided however, with another new development. The administration of many police forces was increasingly being undertaken by civilian staff rather than police officers.

As more officers were required for operational duties, so the administrative functions of police forces were in the hands of civilian staff. Inevitably, this led to civilians, especially those working closely with pay departments, supporting the Force Authorised Officers.

A civilian employee could not become a member of the PMAS, simply because he or she was not a police officer. It also raised the question of their attendance at the annual general meeting. Even if such a person was an authorised officer, the fact that he or she was not a police officer and therefore not a member of the Society, meant that he or she could neither vote nor take any active part in the proceedings. They could attend merely as observers. It was a problem which was to recur several times in the years to follow and it did lead to questions as to why a civilian employee, especially one whose work included the duties of an authorised officer, could not become a member of the PMAS.

In 1970 the PMAS received yet another request to admit other officers as members; this time it came from the British Airports Authority Constabulary. The PMAS responded that it would be happy to admit such officers as members of the Society, provided that the Authority agreed to deduct their premiums at source from pay. The Authority said it would be happy to do so – but on 2½% commission! The PMAS rejected this suggestion and so the BAAC asked if its members could pay by bankers' order into a special account. This would be maintained at its Force HQ and would be the responsibility of the authorised officer. To this, the PMAS agreed.

It was in 1971 that Sir John McKay, CBE, QPM, MA, HM Chief Inspector of Constabulary was nominated to succeed Sir Eric St Johnston as President of the PMAS. Sir Eric was to retire after a remarkable career.

Tension was building up both nationally and within the walls of Alexandra House with the approach of the date of decimalisation of the British currency in 1971 which was also the date of the Golden Jubilee of the PMAS, but another problem was that the

PMAS loan scheme, previously hailed as a boon to many officers, was encountering some difficulties. With a general increase in interest rates, it was realised that some borrowers were in fact being subsidised by the Society, a state of affairs that could not continue. Furthermore, some borrowers had changed address without notifying the PMAS, thus making the collection of repayments very difficult. In addition, the loan scheme was becoming uneconomic to administer and a further factor was that the reason for its introduction (difficulties in obtaining bank loans) had now disappeared.

A combination of these factors meant that the future of the loan scheme was in jeopardy. After much discussion, it was decided to phase out this scheme, no further loans being granted after lst January 1972. Exceptional individual cases might be considered on merit, but the general scheme was therefore brought to an end. Nonetheless, new schemes were being considered, perhaps the most important and far-reaching of which was the House Purchase plan.

In the autumn of 1970, the Society reported discussions with a sub-committee of the Police Federation which had resulted in the belief that a joint PMAS/Police Federation House Purchase scheme was feasible. The Secretary was asked to examine the proposal in greater depth. Another proposed new scheme was COP – the Convertible Option Policy. This arose when it was realised that, in a rapidly changing society, there was increasing competition in which not all the insurance requirements of a police officer were met with the existing PMAS policies. The COP scheme involved a basic £500 (or multiple of £500) endowment assurance, with profits, either in the 'tax exempt' (concessional) or 'taxable' (extended) scheme.

The policy would be issued with an additional convertible temporary assurance for an identical term, and for a sum assured of at least £500 rising in steps of £500 to £3,000 at an additional premium. The temporary assurance could be converted, in easy stages of £500 units, to an endowment assurance cover without medical evidence during the term of the basic endowment policy, except during the last five years. The Convertible Option Policy was introduced in March 1971 and was an immediate success.

In examining the feasibility of group insurance, they would also consider the introduction of a policy which might replace the old 'Panda' scheme. It was found that the PMAS/Police Federation House Purchase scheme, which owed so much to the expertise of the Society's Head Office staff and the support it received from a number of leading building societies, was an undoubted success and so the range of assurances available from the PMAS was suddenly and rapidly expanded.

Another new scheme which was to follow in 1972 was the Recruits' Special Privilege Scheme. Recruits to the service could automatically be enrolled for a basic £500 endowment policy (with or without a convertible option), within six months of joining the force and without any medical questions. With so many assurance schemes now available, it was important that each functioned at its most efficient and so these were periodically examined by the Consulting Actuary. In March 1972, he scrutinised the Endowment Scheme, the Recruits' Special Privilege Scheme, the Convertible Option Policy, the 'Panda' Scheme, term assurance and the possibility of introducing a Group Life Insurance Scheme, the latter now being permitted under recently introduced legislation. It was, in the event, decided not to continue with a Group Life policy.

But scrutiny of the viability of existing policies revealed that the 'Panda' Scheme, so successful and so popular over the past years, had now run its course.

No longer did it meet the needs of the police service, for the surge in house purchase had led to an increased demand for mortgage protection. The 'Panda' scheme was insufficiently flexible to meet all such needs. To some extent, those needs were met by COP, but it was decided that the 'Panda' policy should be discontinued in its existing form and re-constituted as a genuine mortgage protection policy. This would complement the house purchase scheme which was proving very popular. It was also borne in mind that there was increasing competition from commercial insurance companies. The 'Panda' policy would have to be phased out.

The competition from other insurance companies did create serious debate within the Committee, so much so that one development under discussion was the possible appointment of full-time paid representatives to be engaged on promoting the sales of policies to police officers. These representatives would be members of Head Office staff who would travel to forces to act as salesmen for the PMAS. But this idea was rejected – it was felt that police officers would resist any attempts at high pressure salesmanship, and it would also be a problem speaking to officers when they were on duty, while their private addresses could not be revealed by their force headquarters.

Although it was appreciated that personal contact between Head Office and potential members was desirable, it was decided that it was best left to the existing system.

The contact made by authorised officers and divisional representatives, aided by head office staff visits to training centres, pre-retirement courses and force conferences, was continuing to achieve good results.

With so much activity and change, it is not surprising that the new Head Office was quickly found to be too small and already there was talk of adding an extension. More office space would soon become necessary.

1971, the Jubilee Year of the PMAS, was celebrated with a luncheon at the Savoy Hotel, Blackpool as part of the proceedings at the Annual Conference, but it was also the year of decimalisation of the currency. On Monday 15th February 1971 the nation abandoned its old £.s.d. system of currency in favour of decimal coinage and the PMAS was able to report that the change-over had been effected with remarkable ease and with far less inconvenience than had been envisaged, even though there had been a nationwide postal strike at the time. All its huge bank of personal files, well over 130,000, in addition to its literature, tables of calculation and associated documents had all been converted in time for the nation's change-over.

Meanwhile, the routine work of the Society continued – applications were processed, maturities dealt with, advertising material distributed, meetings held, visits both made and received and plans made for an extension to Alexandra House.

And, as if to add to the pressure in Head Office, there was the onset of Value Added Tax to consider, the effect upon friendly societies of Britain's entry into the EEC (European Economic Community, or Common Market) and, even more daunting, a whole new series of police force amalgamations, along with a reconstitution of county boundaries and changes to Metropolitan county and police areas which were planned for 1974. Another huge re-organisation and amendment of hundreds of thousands of records was thus heralded with the problems that would surely accrue from having to cope with new pay systems, transfers of police personnel and different administrative procedures. Authorised officers would then have to cope with a whole new set of problems.

Meanwhile, the Ministry of Defence Police made an application for its members to be allowed membership and the PMAS made its now familiar response – such an application would be considered if the force permitted premiums to be deducted from pay at source. At first, there was no response to this – the Society had a long wait for the Force to make up its mind. It took six months for the M o D Police to agree to the PMAS terms but it did – and its officers were accepted as members from October 1973.

The next force to make such an application was the City of Manchester Airport Police and again, the PMAS agreed to accept its members if they appointed an authorised officer, and if they would deduct premiums from pay.

The force agreed to these conditions and so, before the end of 1973, its officers were allowed to become members. This was agreed even though it was soon likely that the force would be amalgamated with the British Airports Authority whose officers were already eligible for membership. Meanwhile, individual officers of the British Transport Police continued to make personal efforts to become PMAS members even though their force would not meet the conditions earlier requested by the Society and so the Secretary wrote to the Chief Constable asking him to reconsider the possibility of allowing deductions of premiums from pay. This had been refused in the past but the official response was that BTP officers already had a satisfactory insurance scheme with the Provident Mutual Association, while, in addition, their own Police Federation had a Group Accident Policy. The Chief Constable saw no reason for his officers to become PMAS members.

The Society experienced something of a disappointment when its plans for an office extension were rejected by Staffordshire County Council's Planning Committee but the good news was that the extension might be sanctioned if it was for a single storey building instead of a two-storey construction. New plans were quickly drawn up and this time they were approved.

A single storey office extension to Alexandra House could be built but the Society knew that this would take some time – two years at least – and so the plans were put 'on ice' for a short time, with the intention of having the building finished by, say, the end of 1976. In fact, it was to be much later before the building was eventually extended. In the meantime, Alexandra House won an accolade from the local community – the building was awarded the 1972 Lichfield Civic Society award for the best new building in the city. The citation praised, *inter alia*, the bold design which had produced a building which invited entry and which 'looks as if something is happening inside'.

Things were, and still are happening inside – it's a very busy place. At the end of 1972, the Society's assets had increased yet again, this time to more than £22 million, with premium income surpassing £3 million for the first time. In some ways though, the year had been described as 'traumatic', due in no small way to a pay freeze, run-away inflation, a miner's strike, gas workers' strike, mass unemployment, a railway strike, the first-ever civil servants' strike with protests from teachers and hospital workers – and difficulties by the police in coping with the social unrest which accompanied these disputes. Britain was also accepted as a member of the EEC, the European Economic Community, more popularly known as the Common Market.

Perhaps it was because of the financial problems of the Government that the PMAS received requests for the re-introduction of its loan scheme which had been phased out only a year or so earlier, and this was approved. A revised scheme for temporary loans was therefore approved and welcomed, and this was closely followed by the introduction in January 1973 of a new plan called Moneyspinner. The name of this policy was inspired and it proved to be a huge success, with more than 1000 proposals being received before the year end. It was a simple £1-per-week contract over a ten year period which gave double death benefit with maximum income tax relief on the premiums. The contract could be issued as a convertible option policy so that it could be converted into an endowment. Another form of investment sought by police officers was a means of investing lump sums with the PMAS, something not yet available but which appealed especially to those who commuted part of their pensions. The Society was soon to examine that feasibility too, as it brought to an end the popular 'Panda' policy. This ended in October 1972, having been introduced in September 1967. Almost 23,000 'Panda' policies had been issued for sums assured of around £45 million.

Early in 1973, Sir John McKay retired as President of the PMAS and his place was taken by the new Chief HMI, Mr (later

Sir), John M. Hill, CBE, DFC, QPM, and the Society also recorded with regret the death of the Deputy Chairman of the Committee of Management, Mr John F. Lumley.

He had been a member of the Committee since 1961, having served with great distinction, particularly in his capacity as a member of the Building Sub-Committee. In his place, Chief Superintendent J.R. Furber was elected Deputy Chairman with Chief Inspector P. Simpson becoming the Assistant Deputy Chairman. The Society suffered a further loss too that year, with the death of the former Chairman, Mr E.S. Drake on 13th December 1973. His service with the PMAS had spanned more than 42 years.

The Society extended its commitment to new technology with the purchase of a further NCR Accounting Machine and later introduced archival micro-filming as a means of reducing storage space for files and records as they faced conference problems due to the effects of petrol rationing. The 1974 Annual Conference was due to be held in Llandudno on 7th and 8th May and there was concern that rationed petrol supplies would make it difficult for delegates to attend. Research, however, showed that the resort had an excellent rail service from all parts of Britain and so the venue was allowed to stand. As it transpired, no petrol rationing problems arose.

As part of its publicity activities, the PMAS decided that its popular little booklet, 'Police Definitions' should be phased out and replaced by another one incorporating police powers. Initially, the booklet was restricted solely to a collection of police powers but it was later extended to include police definitions as well as police powers.

The new booklet received an enthusiastic response, especially from training centres and it was in 1974 that the Society ventured into its first attempt at sponsorship.

It received a letter from the Chief Constable of Gwynnedd Constabulary, Mr P.A. (later Sir Philip) Myers – and a Vice

Pictured during the 1974 Annual Conference at Llandudno
Back Row (left to right) Mr. W. Baharie (ACC, Northumbria), Mr. T. R. Davies, Mr. J. Haughton (CC, Merseyside), Mr. J. W. Hadley, Mr. D. Gray (HM Chief Inspector of Constabulary for Scotland), Mr. A. F. King, Sir Derek Capper (CC, West Midlands), Sir Graham Shillington (former CC, RUC), Mr. S. Parr (CC, Lancashire), Mr. P. A. Myers (CC, North Wales), Mr. J. P. Hughes (Chief Executive, Aberconwy District Council)
Front Row Mr. J. Wright (Chairman), Councillor C. R. Payne (Mayor), Sir John Hill (President), Mr. J. B. Flanagan (CC, RUC), Mr. A. M. Rees (CC, Staffordshire), Sir Williams Jones Williams (formerly CC, North Wales)

President of the Society – who announced that his force wished to organise a new event for police cadets, beginning in September 1974. It was to be a type of endurance contest open to all forces in England and Wales, and it would comprise teams of four cadets who would cover a 13-mile route which incorporated all seven peaks in the Snowdonia range.

The contest, to be known as the Snowdonia Seven, would be a test of endurance, stamina and team spirit and all forces were to be invited to enter two teams of cadets. At the same time, it was pointed out that police cadets also took part in rugby football and soccer contests and there was a suggestion that the PMAS might also sponsor some of those such as, for example, the National Cadet Five-A-Side Soccer competition to be held for the first time during the 1974–5 season. After due consideration, the Society decided not to sponsor the various rugby football or soccer competitions, but it did agree to act as sponsor for the

Snowdonia Seven event, and to donate a trophy or shield for the winning team as well as other suitable awards. When the recruiting of cadets diminished, this event was suspended for two years, but it was revived and extended to include regular officers as well as cadets.

The number of teams also increased and the competition was extended to include veterans in 1986. It continues to attract a large entry and maintains a very high standard.

It was in 1974 that another vexed issue was raised yet again, one which would continue to be raised for many years. Women police officers asked if their husbands, who were not police officers, could become members of the PMAS. It was a long established practice for the wives of serving officers to be admitted to membership but the question of husbands of officers raised a different set of assurance risks. A simple example was a police-woman's husband whose work entailed high risks to his life, something which was not a common element in the life of a policeman's wife. The request was rejected.

Another request for membership from civilians employed by the police authorities was also rejected but a welcome change by police authorities occurred when some agreed to the deduction of

Snowdonia Seven
Mountain Trial

high in the Welsh mountains

the trophies

police pensioners' premiums at source. This, and even the deductions of serving officers' premiums, was to undergo another upheaval on 1st April 1974 in England and Wales, and on 1st May 1974 in Scotland, when the next series of police force amalgamations, and the creation of new counties and Metropolitan police areas, was implemented. New police forces appeared, not very old ones disappeared and new council authorities were created. It meant another massive re-organisation at Head Office and immense changes to the administrative systems of authorised officers.

Many new forces covered larger areas with an increased number of officers which meant bigger divisions and more men to be catered for by the Authorised Officers. The question of assistance for Authorised Officers was again raised and this also prompted the Society to express concern about the delegate representation at the annual conference. Fewer police forces with larger divisions would result in a drop in the number of delegates at conference and this was something already being aggravated by the increase in the number of civilians who were acting as authorised officers. The Society urged police forces to be well represented at the conference and especially by their authorised officers.

In fact, a 1971 change to the PMAS rules on committee representation following the 1968 amalgamations did ensure that each force sent one representative, usually its Authorised Officer and it is now the case that every force is represented at Conference.

One force which was always well represented was the City of London. Its authorised officer, Mr A.E. (Bert) Treves had done the job without a break since May 1939, a total of 35 years – and as we go to press, he remains a Life Vice President, an honour awarded in the presence of his Commissioner, Mr James Page, a former colleague in the ranks, and in 1991 Bert Treves was awarded the Society's first Award of Merit. It was said of him at the time, "He wears the mantle of doyen of the PMAS with dignity – and sparkle!"

And then the Society's Manager & Secretary, Mr J.W. Hadley who in 1974 completed 25 years' service with the PMAS, announced his retirement which was to take effect from 1st July 1975. He had taken over from the noted Captain Wood in September 1954 and was, effectively, therefore only the Society's second Secretary.

Mr. John Hadley with his wife, Joan, and son, Lindsay, upon the occasion of the award of his MBE

His place was taken by Mr Alan F. King, FCII, with Mr Peter Sharpe, FCII as his Deputy and Mr Fred Smith as Assistant. Mr Michael Kilgallen, FCII was shortly to be appointed Assistant Secretary to complement the executive team.

The first meeting of the Committee of Management in 1975 was conducted in a climate of serious national economic difficulties with the added threat of severe inflation under the Labour Government. That meeting, in the January of 1975, was memorable for a further reason – the Committee of Management knew that the Financial Times 30-share Index had plunged to 148, leaving the worth of the Society's investments well below their book value. This discomfiture was shared by many other insurance companies as well as most other financial institutions, large and small. One major British trading company, Burmah Oil, needed Government support in order to survive and in many minds, doubts were expressed about the continuing financial viability of the country's economic future. But as the Society's investments were held over the long term, with no involvement with speculative trading, the Committee of Management was confident that there would be a recovery over the next few months – as indeed there was.

Another factor was the effects of the Health and Safety at Work Act of 1974 which imposed a statutory duty upon employers to safeguard the safety and health of their staff at work. The Society had always maintained these ideals and implementation of the new Act created few, if any, worries.

MR ALAN F. KING,

OBE, FCII

Alan King was educated at King Edward VI Grammar School, Camp Hill. He spent his early career with the Wesleyan & General Assurance Society and during the war earned his wings as a bomber pilot while serving in Canada. He was appointed Assistant Secretary of the Police Mutual in 1954, promoted Deputy Manager & Secretary in 1967, and was appointed Manager & Secretary in 1975, a position he held until 1986.

Mr King's special interests include travel, cricket (President of Lichfield Cricket Club), and the theatre. As Manager & Secretary, Alan King built upon and consolidated the progress to which he himself had contributed over twenty years of working with John Hadley. He will be remembered for his interest in people and a remarkable eye for detail. He insisted upon the highest administrative standards and his service to the police was recognised by the award of the OBE in the 1982 New Year Honours List.

As the new team settled down to their task, Sir Derrick Capper, QPM, the Chief Constable of the West Midlands, retired as a Vice President of the Society, a position he had occupied since 1974, and in his farewell speech urged the Society to make full use of new technology. He highlighted the use of computers and technology within the service as a whole, including the Police National Computer, and advised both the service, and the PMAS, to make use of the very best equipment that was available. It was sound advice which the Society was to heed.

Still hovering above the heads of the new team, however, was the question of admitting to PMAS membership the husbands of women officers. This was again raised – and rejected.

The knotty question of admitting civilian staff to membership also arose – and was rejected.

It was pointed out that not even the staff of the PMAS Head Office could become members, unless they were the wives of policemen or, of course, retired officers who could meet the required conditions. But the repeated demands for husbands of policewomen to be admitted was again raised in the autumn of 1975 and once again rejected. The Society said, "The special position of a wife as being a dependant of her husband is recognised by the Society. Neither in respect of pension nor social security, even under new legislation, is a husband in the same position of dependency as a wife."

The PMAS then received a request from the Merseyside Police Benefit Friendly Society who wished to know whether the PMAS was willing to take over its assets and liabilities but although PMAS declined this opportunity, it did raise the question of whether there was scope for a new type of policy which would take the place of various small schemes which were still being run by several forces throughout the country. In 1976, it was agreed that "Life of Another" contracts were acceptable for all police officers on the life of a spouse and a new low cost Mortgage Endowment policy was also introduced. This anticipated future bonus levels and combined many of the advantages of endowment repayment with a low monthly outlay.

Another innovation was the popular 15-year Prosperity Plan, a contract based on the successful Moneyspinner and providing a package-deal type of savings plan based on premiums of just £1 a week (or multiples of £1), with added death cover.

Proposals for a Hospitalisation scheme, however, were rejected while the Friendly Societies limits for assurance were raised. The new limit was now £10,000 per member which meant that the PMAS could compete for new business on terms which were competitive with those offered by commercial companies.

Even though the police received no pay increase in 1976, the year produced substantial new business as policewomen continued to press for membership on behalf of their husbands and it was the Sex Discrimination Act of 1975 which settled the issue. Rather than make a legal issue out of this question, the Society's Committee of Management, acting on advice from its own solicitor and the General Secretary of the National Conference of Friendly Societies, decided to admit to membership the husbands of serving women police officers. But civilian employees of police authorities were still outside the scope of PMAS membership. They were to continue to press for membership, particularly those who were acting as authorised officers.

Among the others who wished to become members of the PMAS were officers of the newly formed Port of Liverpool Police; they were accepted having fulfilled the Society's conditions, while in other forces, a new development had occurred.

Some authorities were selling disused police houses and quite suddenly, the occupiers of such premises found themselves able to purchase a house at a comparatively modest price.

This, and the general trend towards house purchase by police officers, led to the creation of the PMAS's Low Cost Mortgage Endowment Scheme, which was well received. Meanwhile at Head Office, new mechanised and computerised office systems were being examined. It was necessary, for example, to find a way of stream-lining the issue of certificates and so a 5-man sub-committee, chaired by Mr J. Wright, the former Deputy Chief Constable of Staffordshire, was established to examine the future mechanised needs of Head Office. The process of mechanisation was, even now, well advanced and early in 1977, an NCR 499 Electronic Data Processing System was purchased and installed. All new policies were issued on the new system, and later it would include the preparation of maturity claims.

There were staff changes too – Mr Fred Smith, the long-serving and highly respected Assistant Manager retired on 31st July 1977 and Mr W.F. Moore, ACII was appointed Assistant Secretary. The Society noted, with sadness, the death of Sir Derrick Capper, a strong supporter of the Society.

In 1977, an analysis of the figures for 1976 showed that it had been a remarkable year for new business – new records had been established but as 1977 got underway, it was noted, with some reserve, that there was a falling-off of such business. Premium rates for all classes of policy were reviewed and new schedules ap-proved, but it emerged that there was a serious pay problem for the police.

Under the Labour Government, they had fallen a long way behind in the nation's pay position and the Police Federation was calling for a substantial increase. There was also a reduction in the numbers of cadets being recruited and some forces were to end such recruitment. In 1977, this led to the suspension of the PMAS Snowdonia Seven event in Wales because there were insufficient cadets to take part, and the presentation shield was returned to Head Office for retention, hopefully until the event could be resumed. It was, in fact, re-instated in August 1979, with teams of serving officers as well as cadets being invited to take part.

1978 was yet another year of record progress, particularly in the Society's house purchase department. It was evident that many officers wished to become property owners, and in coping with the surge of work, the new office systems were put to a severe test. They all proved invaluable and in December that same year, there was further mechanisation with the installation of an NCR Visible Record Machine Computer System.

The Society welcomed an eminent guest at its 1978 meeting in Eastbourne. He was Mr Keith Brading, CB, MBE, the Chief Registrar of Friendly Societies who complimented the PMAS along with its staff and Committee of Management upon its high standards and expertise. He was impressed by the investment policy of the Society and disclosed that he had just recommended to HM Treasury that the limits of taxable business should be increased to a more realistic level.

He also floated the suggestion that the PMAS might consider becoming a mutual company – but advised the Society to be aware of both the advantages and disadvantages of such a move. The Friendly Societies life assurance limit was in fact increased, this time to £15,500 and this led to more new forms of assurance being discussed. One was a Joint Life Cover scheme, another was a joint PMAS Building Society Special Savings Plan designed for officers with lump sums to invest, and another was the question of a PMAS Medical Care plan which was also raised. This was rejected because such insurance is of a very specialised nature and would not be a suitable development of PMAS activities. Civilian employees continued, without success, to seek admission as members of the PMAS but police pensioners gained some success with an increase in the limit for their endowment policies.

This was increased to £4,000 and it was reported that more police forces were willing to deduct retired officers' premiums from their pensions. The idea of the joint PMAS/Building Society scheme was to emerge in 1980 under the name of the Capitaliser Scheme, a well received capital sum investment plan.

In March 1979, the Labour Government was defeated and the election of the Conservatives led by Mrs Margaret Thatcher, led to a boost of investment confidence. It also marked another important step forward for the professionalism of the police service.

Since 1977, the Committee of Inquiry on the Police, under its Chairman, the Right Honourable Lord Edmund-Davies, PC, had been sitting and, following pressure from the Police Federation, its terms of reference had been extended to include police pay. In July 1978, the Report (Cmnd 7283) was presented to Parliament and caused an uproar because it recommended a huge pay increase for police officers, with future salary increases being automatically based upon an earnings index. The Labour Government refused to pay the increase, saying it would pay half the recommended amount, but the newly elected Conservative Government agreed to pay the full amount. The outcome for the Society was a large influx of new business as officers revealed a desire to invest their income in the wisest possible way.

This was also followed by changes within the Society. In March 1980, Mr J. Wright, MBE, O St J, QPM, announced his retirement as Chairman of Committee. Mr Wright, a former Deputy Chief Constable of Staffordshire, had given unparalleled service to the PMAS, being a member of its Committee of Management since 1946. He had been an authorised officer and was chairman of the Building Sub-Committee which was responsible for the building of Alexandra House. He was acknowledged as a gracious Chairman of outstanding quality and was succeeded by Mr J.R. Furber, QPM, MIAM, the Assistant Chief Constable of Cheshire Constabulary.

Mr Furber had already demonstrated his qualities as a Chairman in deputising for Mr Wright at the Annual Conferences in 1978 and 1979.

The new Conservative Government had a tremendous amount of corrective work ahead of them and it would take time to restore total confidence in the economy. The year was an uncertain one; then there was a sharp increase in the Minimum Lending Rate (up

MR JOHN R. FURBER, QPM

John Furber is a Salopian by birth but has adopted Cheshire as his home county. He served with the Royal Artillery during the Second World War and joined the Cheshire Constabulary in May 1947.

He served in every Division of that Force, and with experience in both uniform and CID, was promoted Sergeant in 1954. He progressed through the ranks until 1967 when, as Chief Superintendent in charge of Administration, he organised the transfer to the new Headquarters. This was closely followed by the amalgamation of Stockport, Birkenhead and Wallasey Boroughs with the Cheshire Constabulary. He was appointed Assistant Chief Constable of Cheshire in 1977 and retired in June 1982.

He acted as Chairman of the North West Police Benevolent Fund from 1974 to 1981.

In 1976, he was awarded the Queen's Police Medal and was further honoured by being made a Serving Brother of the Order of St John of Jerusalem. Mr Furber's recreational activities include helping out many community groups, gardening and golf.

Mr Furber first became a PMAS Authorised Officer in 1954 and was elected to the Committee of Management in 1967 after serving for two years as a co-opted member. He was appointed Deputy Chairman in 1973 and took over as Chairman in 1980 when he was also elected a Vice President. In 1989, he was appointed a Life Vice President in recognition of his outstanding work for the Society.

to 17% from 12%), VAT was increased from 8% to 15% and share prices fell, but the wisdom of the PMAS Investment Committee prevailed. They had chosen wisely, and the Society's investments continued to grow.

Computerisation of Head Office accounting systems was continuing, even though some regarded the use of computers with more than a little cynicism, and the transfer to computer from the earlier mechanical system was completed on schedule. Alan King, the Manager & Secretary described this gradual computerisation as 'the quiet revolution' and said that every new process should enable the Society to grow and to maintain and improve the high quality of service offered by the PMAS.

To continue that high quality of service, new lines of advertising were being studied and tested, one of which was a portable display stand devised by Sergeant Kenneth Barrell of West Yorkshire. This would be taken from force to force and used to display literature from the PMAS – it was to prove a highly useful device.

The task of making every officer aware of the benefits of the PMAS continued to exercise the minds of the staff at Alexandra House. They did appreciate that the busy police officer has so little time to unravel the complexities of life assurance contracts and it was felt that a high proportion of officers never did appreciate the wide-ranging benefits of PMAS membership. This realisation led to a new business strategy which was designed to attract even more members. The language of the promotional literature would have to be such that the ordinary officer could quickly assess his needs; any interpretation of the technical aspects would be left to Head Office to explain, or guidance could be sought from the Force Authorised Officer or the divisional representatives.

One scheme involved the use of a PMAS enquiry card and a pilot scheme with this card, supported by posters, was put into operation in the West Midlands. The post-paid card could be quickly completed and sent to Head Office as a request for more information.

It was always to the forefront of the minds of the PMAS staff that its policies had to be up-to-date and had to be able to compete with commercial companies while continuing in their specialist role as contracts for police officers. One scheme was to identify potential members by categories, eg. single, married, parents, those living in police property, those aged over 45 and so forth, and then to offer the best policy for a particular officer.

During the research into the best methods of alerting officers to the benefits of the PMAS, it was found that most new business tended to be towards endowment savings with a strong interest in mortgage protection. Officers were keen to become home owners and some were now able to purchase council houses at very favourable prices and so the PMAS house purchase schemes continued to attract members. House purchase and life assurance were means of providing the necessary security that police officers wanted for themselves and their families in an increasingly turbulent Britain – operational officers were facing problems from the IRA, riots in Brixton and Bristol, coping with the Iranian Embassy siege, the aftermath of the Prison Officers' dispute and the special policing requirements of Rhodesia. It became fully independent in April 1980 and is now known as Zimbabwe.

Another type of policy that was sometimes requested by officers was one based on a Whole Life scheme, a plan similar to the one which dated to the very beginnings of the PMAS. The Society's Actuary was asked to examine the feasibility of such a scheme. It required careful research, but by 1982, it had been approved and it became known as the POLICE 4000 policy – it was a life assurance scheme presented in units, each unit providing death cover of £4,000 up to the age of 55. At that age, premiums could cease but cover of £1,000 per unit would continue for life.

It was an attractive scheme, a bargain for young officers and it could be used for mortgage protection, commutation protection and general family protection. Perhaps it was the desire for security that led to yet more records for the PMAS – by the end of

1980, the Society's assets had exceeded £55 million, with income from premiums being over £8.5 million and investment income rising towards £5 million. It was the skills which produced such results that were praised by the Registrar General of Friendly Societies, Mr Keith Brading, CB, MBE, when he addressed the 1981 Annual General Meeting at Torquay. It marked the 60th anniversary of the Society and he described its progress as 're-markable' and complimented the management and staff for their enthusiasm.

By the end of 1981, over 19,000 new policies had been effected with a total of sums assured approaching £100 million – in fact, the sum was £98,731,576. Income from premiums had passed the £10 million mark and the new Capitaliser policy had proved immensely popular. More than £750,000 was invested in this policy during its first six months of availability.

The Society's assets were now more than £60 million and investment income had surpassed the £5 million mark. In the months that followed, word processing equipment was installed at Alexandra House and work began to convert the visual filing system into computerised records.

It was intended to have this completed in 1983, another mammoth task for the administrative staff – there were more than 130,000 members' files and over 230,000 policy files to adapt.

At the end of 1982, Mr Gordon Blyth, Superintendent (Systems), retired from Head Office staff. In a relatively short period of eight years' service with the PMAS, he had contributed greatly to the computerisation of the Society's systems and the preparation of the forthcoming on-line system which was soon to be installed. The programme for the conversion of existing files to a data processing system was placed in the care of a small working party, with a provisional timetable beginning in March 1982. Stage 1 would be complete by the end of 1983 and that comprised computerisation of all policy files, members' files, new business, claims, head office accounts, cheque writing, actuarial valuation and some correspondence. Stage 2, planned to go 'live' in January 1984, would include management accounts and other ledgers. By February 1983, a suitable system had been installed and so began the enormous task of converting files and accounts.

Thirty extra but temporary staff with the necessary skills were recruited to effect the change-over and the existing staff in Head Office had then to be trained in the use of the new technology, including visual display units and printers.

Some of the Society's equipment in the 1970's. The photographs show the revolving filing consoles and early computer equipment

It was a mammoth task which involved more than 360,000 files while the work of the Society continued in what was to become an astonishingly busy and successful year. It is to the credit of all involved that all deadlines were met and the system went 'live' with Stage 1 in August 1983, which was the intended date.

The pace of change was accelerating and a beneficial new development in income tax relief on house purchase was introduced. This was called MIRAS which meant 'Mortgage Interest Relief at Source' and this would substantially benefit many new house buyers and indeed many existing owners who cared to adopt the MIRAS system of tax relief. The result was literally an explosion of enquiries. Staff in the house purchase department at

Alexandra House were swamped with requests for information, these numbering between 1,000 and 1,500 per week for a considerable period. It resulted in a special MIRAS department being established in Head Office and the net result was a flow of new business that superseded anything previously experienced in the long history of the Society. The Society was able to channel the twin merits of its own policies and those of the MIRAS system to the benefit of its members.

More business resulted from yet another increase in the assurance limits for members of friendly societies – it was now raised to £50,500 per person or £101,000 for a husband and wife jointly insured.

And all the other policies were proving popular.

It is not surprising that 1983 was another record year in which the volume of new business was outstanding – annual premiums rose by a staggering 48.06% while sums assured rose by more than 33%. Assets of the Society soared above £90 million while the level of income from premiums increased to £13,939,005 and from investments (after tax) to £7,089,869.

Committee of Management and officers 1983
Back Row: Messrs. D. G. H. Smith, D. B. Humphries, M. J. Kilgallen, B. E. Wallis, W. R. Parry, R. B. Thomas, A. Ross, P. J. Sharpe, W. J. Newton
Middle Row: Messrs. R. E. Lamb, J. G. Bentley, P. Simpson, A. F. King, K. M. McKelvey, A. Leach
Front Row: Messrs. A. E. Treves, J. Wright, J. R. Furber (Chairman), Sir James Crane (President) and Sir George Terry

It was during 1983 that Mr Furber retired from his post as Assistant Chief Constable (Administration) of Cheshire Constabulary but he continued to serve as Chairman of the PMAS Committee of Management. Sir James Crane also retired from his post as HM Chief Inspector of Constabulary and he was succeeded by Mr Lawrence Byford, CBE, QPM, LLB who was elected President of the Police Mutual Assurance Society. He was later to become Sir Lawrence Byford. On the staff, Mr M. J. Pate was appointed Assistant Manager and the Society received yet another application from a police force – on this occasion, it was the International Police of Gibraltar, a small force with a strength of only 230 officers. Their pay, duties and conditions of service were very similar to those of UK officers but the rules of the PMAS did not cater for such forces.

They encompassed police forces in England, Wales, Scotland, Northern Ireland, the Isle of Man, Jersey and Guernsey but the Committee decided to examine the Gibraltar request in detail.

It was decided, however, with some reluctance, that the existing rules did not permit membership by officers of this force.

At the end of the year, the range of policies offered by the PMAS was infinitely wider than the two schemes it had administered in 1922 – and one of those had been inherited from the old Police Mutual Assurance Association. Now, there was a choice of nine different schemes, one of which had two alternatives which made a selection of ten.

For the record, those types of policy were as follows:
Endowment with Profits
Convertible Option
Low-Cost Mortgage Endowment
10-year Moneyspinner
15-year Prosperity Plan
Mortgage Protection
    (a)   With return
    (b)   Without return

Special Term Assurance
Unit Trust Endowment
POLICE 4000

Changes brought about by new legislation and the Budget were to amend the benefits of some – for example, the tax exemption limit was raised to £750 by the Budget in March, 1984; the maximum sum assured permitted to friendly society members was increased yet again, this time to £60,750 per member (£121,500 for husband and wife) while in May 1984, the allowance for nomination was raised to £5,000. This allowed members to nominate beneficiaries other than themselves to receive benefits from their policies, and at the same time, the Administration of Estates (Small Payments) Act increased its limit from £1,500 to £5,000. This therefore enabled the PMAS to widen its scope to make death claim settlements with the minimum of formality – but within a year, the £60,750 limit imposed on friendly society members was to be abolished completely by the Friendly Societies Act of 1984.

Within a year, that is by February 1985, there was no limit to the sum assured which was allowed for each member of a friendly society, and so the PMAS promptly set about advertising the enormous expansion of its policies.

But 1984 was not the easiest of years. Until March of that year, holders of life assurance policies had been able to pay their premiums net of Life Assurance Premium Relief (LAPR), the then current rate being 15%, but the Government withdrew this tax concession for any new policies issued after that date. It was generally felt that this could have an adverse effect on applications for new life assurance policies, but for friendly societies, it was moderated by the extension in tax exemption announced at the same time. In fact, there was a slight reduction in the numbers of new policies issued and this might have also been due to a slowing down or a reduction in the numbers of recruits being admitted to the service, or it might have been a natural reduction after the dramatic increase of business in 1983, or it might have been due in part to the effects of the miners' strike of that year.

It is probable that several factors were involved. Many authorised officers were on duty during the strike and their removal, albeit temporarily to operational duties, meant that they were not in a position to fully undertake their normal work, part of which included voluntary services to the PMAS. In some forces, pre-retirement courses had been cancelled and so the traditional means of achieving contact between the PMAS and police officers had, for the time being, been curtailed. And it did have some effect at Alexandra House where the resultant reduction in the volume of business was noticed. But this was a temporary matter and once the strike was over, normal business was resumed.

The PMAS continued with its advertising and publicity policies and coped with yet another repeated request that civilian employees of the police service be admitted. This was rejected yet again with reluctance, and another application was received from special constables. It was also rejected.

Meanwhile, the Society had produced another exciting policy, this one being a lump sum investment scheme known as the Capital Growth Bond. It was launched in September 1984 with the objective of providing both income and growth over a specified term.

Although introduced with some low-key publicity, the scheme was popular because it offered two distinct opportunities – (a) the income bond appealed to retiring officers who wished to invest part of their pension commutation to provide an income with the added prospect of some capital growth and (b) the growth bond attracted both serving and retired officers who wished to make a lump sum investment with growth possibilities.

In spite of being so busy and so successful, the PMAS continued in its drive to attract yet more members and while appreciating that a membership drive which was too commercial would not be welcomed by police officers, it did produce some attractive ideas. One was a 'news-sheet' which would be called *Lifeline;* it would be produced by the PMAS Head Office staff and would contain articles and photographs of personal and professional interest, along with any news items, details of new developments and legal changes likely to affect members as well as personal pieces about Head Office staff, their social and sporting activities and news from authorised officers. The magazine would appear regularly and 20,000 copies would be printed for circulation to all police forces through their authorised officers. It was a good idea and the response was heart-warming, for it did result in closer liaison between Head Office and the membership while simultaneously leading to an increase in new business. It was launched at the 1985 Annual Conference held on 15th May at the Palace Hotel, Torquay.

That conference was noteworthy for two other features. One was the stirring address given by the President, Sir Lawrence Byford, HM Chief Inspector of Constabulary. He acknowledged that the preceding year had been a very difficult one for the police service, one which had led to criticism of the way in which officers had policed the miners' strike and the picket lines.

He said, "Constructive, justifiable criticism is accepted and corrective action is taken wherever necessary, but constant, negative carping promulgated by vociferous minorities with dubious motives can be a destructive force which in time can undermine the public's faith and distort the true picture."

He went on to say that he had no hesitation in claiming that the British Police Service is the most professional in the world and internationally acknowledged to be so. It was a stirring and heart-warming speech which is too lengthy to be included here, but which will be remembered for a long time.

The second matter which was discussed at this conference was the question of widening the scope for membership of the Society. Over the preceding years, bodies other than the British police service had made requests for admission to the Society and all had been rejected. The Society had commissioned a report and it was presented by Mr Alan King, the Manager & Secretary. He acknowledged that the police service now depended heavily upon the appointment of civilian staff to posts previously held by police officers.

These included many clerical posts and others, such as welfare officers, accident prevention officers, specialists in photography, press officers and many more. Many of them worked in the pay departments and therefore undertook the duties of authorised officers; indeed some were authorised officers and provided sound guidance to police men and women on matters appertaining to the PMAS. Members of the Special Constabulary also carried the responsibilities and obligations of police officers when on duty, and with the cut-back in recruiting, there could only be an increase in civilian staff, and more use made of the Special Constabulary. Many police officers would welcome a relaxation of the rules to permit membership of those who so readily helped them, particularly those who administered the PMAS at force level. Strong arguments were put forward in support of admitting both members of the civilian staff and the Special Constabulary.

Pictured at a Committee of Management meeting in January 1986 (right to left) Sir Lawrence Byford (President) with Mr. R. B. Thomas (CC, Dyfed-Powys), Mr. A. Morrison (HM Chief Inspector of Constabulary for Scotland) and Mr. C. McLachlan (CC, Nottinghamshire) — all Vice Presidents

But problems could be envisaged. Would some members of the civilian staff be admitted and others denied membership? If a clerk was admitted, should a driver, mechanic, cleaner or other civilian employee also be admitted? How could such a distinction be made? And would everyone agree to deductions from their pay? How could Special Constables pay their premiums when they were not on the force pay-roll? And many special constables were engaged in full-time work which may increase the risks attached to them.....

The report was far-reaching and sympathetic to the requests from civilian staff and Specials, but it concluded by saying, *"It is considered that the Society has the capability to develop strongly in the foreseeable future within the service itself, continuing, as has been our practice, to adapt to the changing providential needs of police personnel and the Committee may take the view that so long as this formula proves to be successful, the question of admitting civilians and members of the Special Constabulary may be kept on the sidelines."*

It was regarded as not being an outright rejection, but an acknowledgement that, with the passage of time, both members of the civilian staff of the police service and members of the Special Constabulary might be considered for membership of the PMAS – but not just yet! It was pointed out that the Society had been founded specifically for police officers and their spouses; it was, after all, their very own Society.

Another similar aspect was also to surface. Should co-habiting partners be allowed membership? If wives and husbands of members were permitted to become members, should the facility be offered to the partners who were not married? There had been an increase in the demand for mortgage assurance facilities from co-habiting partners but it was pointed out that the existing Friendly Society legislation permitted assurance to members only on their own lives and the lives of their spouses.

That rule had not been changed and for that reason, applications from co-habiting partners could not be accepted. If that old rule could not be changed, then other changes were afoot within the Society.

The implementation of the Data Protection Act of 1984 prompted the Society to apply for registration, while amendments to the Police Pension Regulations enhanced the need for commutation protection through the PMAS. The changes meant that officers who joined after 8th August 1961 would still be able to retire on ordinary police pension upon the completion of 25 years' pensionable service, but they would not be able to draw their pension, or commute any part of it, until they attained the age of 50 years or completed 30 years' pensionable service. This would create a 'pension freeze' for many who had joined the service before reaching 20 years of age and so, if an officer wished to retire after 25 years, he could have up to five years without receiving his pension.

Clearly, a PMAS policy designed to provide some capital to fill that possible gap would be a welcome bonus! A PMAS endowment policy maturing upon the completion of 25 years' service would be most useful and the Society decided to publicise that facility in its new promotional programme. One aspect of that was the booklet of *Police Definitions and Police Powers*. It had been so successful and with the changes brought about by the Police and Criminal Evidence Act 1984, it would prove itself of even greater value – but it was revealed that a good many of its contents were not applicable to Scotland. Surely a Scottish edition was justified? The Committee of Management agreed that a Scottish edition was a viable suggestion.

Meanwhile, changes were necessary at Alexandra House. Due to the variety of business now being conducted and the sheer volume of work, more computerisation or a major upgrading was needed, more word processors had to be purchased, and the offices had to be re-organised or even extended.

One of the computer systems was known as TOPIC. This was installed in July 1986, and it gives instant access to up-to-the-minute information on Stock Exchange dealings and share prices, both in the United Kingdom and overseas. The Society's day-to-day investments are shown on a screen, together with the buying and selling prices and these are continuously updated, with restrictions on the size of deals being highlighted. This computer gives 24-hour trading information from across the world and it does so on a time-zone basis.

For example, the equity trading day begins in Tokyo, then moves to London after the Far Eastern market closes, and the daily

The Stock Exchange computer which provides a link between the PMAS fund managers and the Stock Market

cycle is completed with New York and other North American markets. TOPIC has given the PMAS instant access to the world's markets and is a huge asset to its day-to-day fund management.

A Stock Market revolution also occurred in 1986.

This was the de-regulation of the Stock Exchange which was effective from 27th October 1986, and which was nicknamed Big Bang. It expanded the eligibility for membership of the Stock Exchange and allowed the big institutions like UK and foreign banks to carry out stock-broking and market making activities.

Commission, previously calculated on fixed rates dependent upon the size of the deal, could now be negotiated. From the point of view of the PMAS, these changes were welcomed because the increased competition resulted in lower charges being paid to its stockbrokers; there were more competitive buying-and-selling prices, plus the ability to deal in larger amounts, all of which combined to provide greater benefits to all PMAS members.

As these changes were being brought into effect, plans for an office extension, approved but not yet implemented, were revived – and then Alan King, the popular and highly competent Manager & Secretary announced his intention to retire. He set the date as the end of November 1986. His intention was noted with great reluctance and it coincided with the retirement of five members of the Committee of Management, one of whom was Mr Peter Simpson, QPM, a former Assistant Chief Constable of West Yorkshire.

He had also been appointed Authorised Officer for the West Riding Constabulary in 1956 and continued in this role until 1986, by which time changes to force boundaries had re-named his force as the West Yorkshire Metropolitan Police. Mr Simpson became a member of the General Committee of the PMAS and was elected to the Committee of Management in 1968. He was appointed Deputy Chairman in 1980 and retired from the Committee of Management and from police service in 1986, having

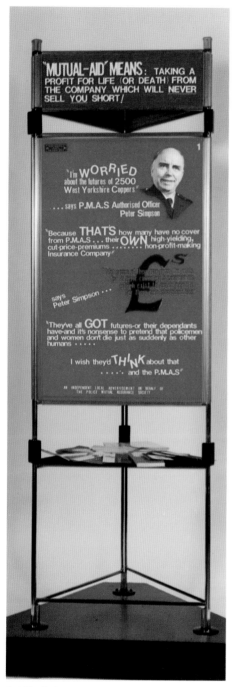

attained the rank of Assistant Chief Constable. He was awarded the Queen's Police Medal in 1983 but sadly died on 29th October 1990 aged 63.

Mr King's impending retirement also coincided with publication of the Financial Services Bill. If this was enacted, it would radically affect the proceedings of institutions such as the PMAS because it sought to establish a framework of investor protection through a number of self-regulatory organisations which were responsible to the Securities and Investments Board.

One of those self-regulatory organisations (SROs) covering the operations of life assurance companies and friendly societies was to be the Life Assurance and Unit Trust Regulatory Organisation, known as LAUTRO. When the Bill became law, a society such as the PMAS could only continue to market its products after it had been authorised to do so by LAUTRO.

This entailed becoming a member of LAUTRO which in turn would require total revision of the Society's literature, itself a costly operation, but another more important factor was that the new regulations appeared designed for commercial companies with salesmen, and they seemed inappropriate for the PMAS and its unpaid authorised officers.

Indeed, would the new regulations allow the continuance of authorised officers in their present form? The Society decided that it must make due representation to the secretariat of LAUTRO so that its unique service and practices could be maintained.

Portable display stand designed and made by Sergeant Kenneth Barrell of West Yorkshire Police

The new Manager & Secretary would have to deal with this and many other problems and so the Committee of Management was faced with the task of finding a replacement for Alan King. His responsibilities would be substantial, not only due to the amount of money and investment for which he was responsible but also for the proper conduct of the whole of the Society's affairs from its staff relations to its continuing function as the country's largest private membership assurance society.

In considering the qualities and qualifications necessary in such a person, the Committee knew they need look no further than Head Office itself. Peter J. Sharpe, FCII, the incumbent Deputy Manager, had already shown his mettle and his capabilities were never in doubt. In the view of the Committee of Management, he was the ideal successor to Mr King.

He was therefore appointed Manager & Secretary, with Mr M. J. Kilgallen, FCII as the Deputy Manager, Mr M. J. Pate, FCII as Deputy Secretary and Mr I.V. Dempster, BA, as Assistant Secretary.

With this formidable and highly skilled team in command, the PMAS was now to be developed and guided towards the 1990s.

The Chairman receives the keys to an investment property in Taunton following its purchase and refurbishment by the Society. Shown here are (left to right) Mr. D. L. Bates (Managing Director of the Contractors), Mr. A. F. King (Manager & Secretary), Mr. J. R. Pool (Surveyor) and Mr. J. R. Furber (Chairman)

MR PETER J. SHARPE,
FCII

At the time of publication of this book, Peter Sharpe is the current General Manager of the Police Mutual Assurance Society. He was educated at King Edward VII Grammar School, King's Lynn, and spent his early career with the Norwich Union Insurance Society. He was appointed Assistant Secretary of the PMAS in 1967 and promoted to Deputy Manager & Secretary in 1975. He took over the position of Chief Executive in 1986. Mr Sharpe is a keen sportsman and has played hockey for Norfolk, Nottinghamshire, Staffordshire, the Midlands and the England 'B' team. He also played minor county cricket for Norfolk. A qualified senior hockey coach and former President of the Midlands Counties Hockey Association, he is currently Chairman of the England Selectors and of the Hockey Association's International Teams' Committee. As General Manager of the PMAS, Peter Sharpe led the restructuring and development of the Society following the de-regulation of the financial services industry.

SELECTED CONTRIBUTIONS

In assembling information for inclusion in this book, we approached many people who were, or who had been, associated with the PMAS over the years. Most of their memories and reminiscences are included within the text, but it was felt that some contributions were worthy of reproduction in their entirety.

One came from John Duncombe, a partner at Wragge and Co., who are long-standing solicitors to the Society. Mr Duncombe specialises in property investment matters and his comments are an insight into some of the characters associated with it.

"My role has often involved liaison with the Chief Executive of the Society, particularly as property is both an expensive and complicated commodity.

It is said that things stem from the top, and therefore the Society must generally reflect the attitudes of the men who lead it from time to time, who have always gone to great lengths to combine both a business-like and very friendly approach. I have often noticed that this atmosphere pervades the Society and one can't help but compare it with one's other successful clients where, more often than not, the same ingredient is to be found.

It is no coincidence that civility and efficiency go together and the running of the Society, from the top downwards, seems to be based on this principle. Coupled with an obvious attention to detail, these factors create an inevitable path to progress.

Senior officers at conferences create a strong impression, particularly the Presidents. I shall always remember the speech of Sir James Crane at Torquay in the ballroom after the band of the Royal Marines had marched and played – on the day the Government had threatened the Marines with severe cutbacks. His rousing theme was the great fighting history of the Marines and his eloquence was so strong that I noticed that a young bandsman in the back row finished up quite literally in tears.

Dinner with Sir Jack Hermon of the RUC was quite an experience when, one night, he completely spoofed the whole

171

table into believing some quite ridiculous story about some out-landish products being made in Belfast. One got the impression that his very strong sense of humour kept him sane to withstand the terrible pressures of his job. What a character!"

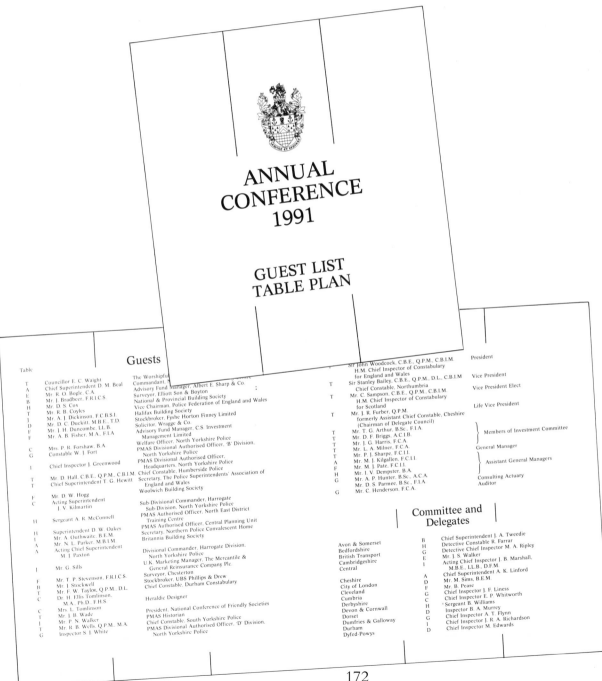

CHAPTER 5

INTO THE 1990's

1987 – 1992

Under its new leadership, the PMAS began to look ahead, not only to the months to come, but towards the end of the 20th century. Although the Society was so well established, it could not settle back and be complacent. It had to show keen but sensitive marketing aggression and it had to convince its potential members that it offered, and could continue to offer, the finest possible investment opportunities for police officers. Those opportunities came in four main categories – savings, protection, house purchase and lump sum investment, but the message about the benefits of each and every one of these had to be repeated to each new intake of police officers as well as to those who had not yet been convinced of the benefits of wise investment.

Peter Sharpe, the new Manager & Secretary summed it up as follows:

"Great changes lay ahead for the PMAS, as well as other financial services and the country as a whole. The Conservative Government led by Mrs Margaret Thatcher was at the height of its powers and its reforming zeal was making an impact on virtually every aspect of British society. Doctors, stockbrokers, trade unionists, schools, local government, building societies, the police – none was left untouched.

It was a period which challenged the PMAS to review its methods of operation and management. In particular, the professional advisers from other organisations who had traditionally assisted with the management of the Society now found that their own organisations were being subjected to considerable change. It was an era of de-regulation – gone was the time when banks were solely concerned with banking, when auditors dealt solely with auditing and when building societies dealt solely with lending money for house purchase. The Society's auditors and consulting actuaries were to be involved in major mergers and the PMAS associated stockbrokers and surveyors were also to become involved with mergers, take-overs and re-organisation."

Mr Sharpe realised that the PMAS must make a careful and considered review of its current situation as well as its future mode of progress. Highly important and far-reaching decisions would have to be made, particularly relating to the independent professional advice which, until now, had been so readily available to the Society and its Committee of Management. Other questions which addressed themselves concerned the management structure at Head Office, the huge responsibility of managing the ever-increasing and substantial funds of the Society and the vexed question of the need for yet more office accommodation. The future of the Society now depended more than ever upon the professionalism of everyone involved – and more than a little goodwill!

By the end of 1986, there was a buoyant demand for the services of the PMAS, dominated by the lively market for mortgages and the high demand for investment savings schemes. 1986 was a year of low inflation, low oil prices and low interest rates in which very selective and wise purchases and sales of ordinary shares were made by the Investment Committee. It was during this year that the Society said farewell to Mr W. J. Newton, the PMAS auditor from the firm of Arthur Young, and this ended some sixty years personal association with the PMAS – Mr Newton's father had also been associated with the Society.

In the early months of 1987, the recently upgraded computer was functioning well, a new telephone system was installed at Alexandra House and some of the schemes offered by the Society were under review.

It was at this time that another fundamental challenge was facing the PMAS. Was it possible to successfully run a sizeable financial institution like the PMAS while retaining effective control in the hands of its police membership bearing in mind the increasing complexity of modern fiscal matters? Certainly, it was no longer possible to expect police officers to play any part in the day-to-day professional management of the Society, nor was it appropriate for them to do so – this point was clearly emphasised in a Government Green Paper on the future of friendly societies. But if the special and unique nature of the PMAS was to be maintained, then the continuing interest and involvement of police officers was essential.

They were needed to complement the professional management of their very own Society and it is fortunate that both the Chairman, Mr John Furber, and the Manager, Mr Peter Sharpe, had a clear understanding of the problems involved.

John Furber retained a deep appreciation of the nature of the police service and the needs of its members but at the same time, he demonstrated total confidence in the new Manager and his ideas. Peter Sharpe has openly acknowledged the encouragement and support he received from the Chairman at a time when many speedy and difficult decisions had to be taken. In taking those decisions, Mr Sharpe was guided by one over-riding consideration, one which has dominated the PMAS since its inception – the financial welfare of its members.

In maintaining that difficult balance between the highest professional standards and the very unique identity of the PMAS, the Chairman and the Manager found themselves working harmoniously and with immense understanding and confidence in one another. Their joint role was a personification of that essential balance which was, and still is, so necessary for a society like the PMAS. Much valued additional support came from the President, the Vice Presidents and elected members of the Committee of Management; this wide cross-section of ranks was unstinting in support and encouragement as Peter Sharpe embarked on a radical review of the management structure at Head Office.

One outcome of this would be that individual executives would be given responsibility for clearly defined areas within the

Society's overall activity, and because there was so much to be achieved without disrupting the Society's service to its members, those changes had to be simultaneous.

They came at a time when there were also impending legislative and regulatory changes and it was recognised that, in spite of the upheaval that must surely follow, the Society's members must be given priority. The task of maintaining liaison with members was made the responsibility of Mr Michael Kilgallen while Mr Michael Pate was charged with the responsibility of coping with new legislation. Both men were to make a major contribution to effecting the foundations of the Society's future.

Mr. Michael Kilgallen addressing a Pre-Retirement Course

Meanwhile, the news-sheet *Lifeline* was proving a highly effective means of communication between Head Office and members of police forces, and some new types of promotional material were being considered such as PMAS tie pins, lapel badges, six-inch rulers, book marks, golf tees and golf markers, all of which offered an effective means of bringing the name of the PMAS to a wider audience. The Society then received yet another request from an overseas police force, this time the Falklands Islands

Police. Their officers wished to have the opportunity to become members of the PMAS, but their application was politely rejected because the rules did not allow membership by overseas forces.

Sadly, the 24 officers and 10 reservists of the Falklands Police Force would have to place their investments elsewhere.

One important factor which dominated the thoughts of both the staff of Alexandra House and the Committee of Management was the overall effect of the Financial Services Act 1986 which set out a framework for the protection of investors and which was to have far-reaching consequences for all financial institutions.

Under the Act, a regulatory body, the Securities and Investments Board (SIB) was established to carry out its provisions. A number of self-regulatory organisations (SROs) were established for different areas of the financial services industry, and these were responsible to the SIB. The Self-Regulatory Organisation for the marketing operations of insurance companies, unit trusts and friendly societies was the Life Assurance and Unit Trust Regulatory Organisation, known as LAUTRO. To be able to continue marketing its schemes, the PMAS had to be authorised by LAUTRO or, alternatively, directly by SIB.

One very practical, expensive and time-consuming outcome was that the majority of forms and proformae used by the PMAS would have to be altered and reprinted. The matter of the Society's unique, unpaid representatives, the authorised officers, had yet to be resolved (see previous chapter) but after studied consideration of the merits of either joining LAUTRO or alternatively seeking approval for its operational functions from SIB, the Securities and Investments Board, the Committee of Management decided to apply for provisional membership of LAUTRO.

Among the draft regulations were those designed to prevent marketing excesses within the sphere of life assurance and these were aimed specifically at full-time paid life assurance representatives, particularly those who received large commissions upon effecting a policy sale.

In due course, all life assurance companies would receive a visit from the compliance enforcement staff of LAUTRO which would, in fact, be in an advisory capacity. This would enable the Head Office staff to discuss the more complex rules of LAUTRO and so the visit was welcomed, even if it did result in some adjustments to current procedures. The first such visit was scheduled for November 1988.

As Mr Sharpe said in his first address to Conference as Manager & Secretary, *"Some of the more dubious marketing methods such as the quoting of outlandish bonus projections and estimated returns will be outlawed by the new consumer protection legislation, but there will be new marketing tricks. During the next few months, young police officers will be at risk as various organisations and their salesmen make a play for their pension contributions as they attempt to woo them away from what is possibly the best pension scheme in the country."*

Mr Sharpe went on to add that *"It is easy to fool some of the people some of the time, but we must operate in a way which will enable us to look our members in the eye in ten or fifteen years from now. If we lose our integrity, we lose everything."*

This aspect apart, however, the entire tone of all the regulations was most complex and it was due to the efforts of the Society's Deputy Secretary, Mr Michael Pate, that a close understanding of those rules had been achieved.

From what was known at that early stage, the new regulations would affect the PMAS in the following areas:

(a) its marketing literature;
(b) a statement would have to be sent to each member who made application for assurance. That statement must accurately outline the benefits, bonuses etc.
(c) the giving of advice by authorised officers and the staff of Head Office would also be affected.

Great care and a high degree of detailed accuracy was demanded in such advice and the PMAS decided to present its marketing literature in terms which were as simple as possible.

Studies of the LAUTRO proposals indicated that one effect was that organisations would have to take responsibility for individual representatives who gave advice about investments, and such representatives would have to operate within a firm set of rules and a code of conduct specified by LAUTRO.

There were precise guidelines on the manner in which the 'product', i.e. the life assurance or investment contract, was described and this attempted to ensure that no inflated or false claims were made about bonuses, surrender values or future projections. There was also going to be a 'cooling off' period during which the potential member could change his or her mind.

LAUTRO was, however, to show itself to be sympathetic to friendly societies and to the PMAS in particular; LAUTRO said, for example, that friendly societies were exempt from the LAUTRO complaints procedure and that their representatives need not be registered with LAUTRO provided they earned less than £500 a year from 'selling' contracts. Authorised officers, of course, earning nothing from the PMAS.

Such representatives must also be of good character, aptitude and competence. The PMAS pointed out that as most of its authorised officers were police officers and some were civilians employed by the police authorities, the question of their character was never in doubt.

Having studied and discussed all aspects of PMAS membership of LAUTRO, the Committee of Management decided to make a formal application to join. There would be a short gap between their application and LAUTRO's decision.

Among the other new legislation affecting the work of the PMAS were new pensions regulations which affected both staff and police officers, plus the implementation of the European Communities Life Directive. This was more formally known as The Friendly Societies (Long Term Insurance Business) Regulations, 1987 which would take effect from 1st January 1988, and so implement for friendly societies, the First Direct Life Assurance

Directive adopted by the Council of European Communities. For the PMAS, this impressive sounding provision meant the removal of restrictions upon its powers to invest its funds, but it did impose annual actuarial valuations, instead of the prevailing triennial valuation.

In fact, the final regulations were yet to be made so the PMAS had to await its provisions. It was known, however, that compliance with the Directive, when implemented, would entail a large amount of unproductive administrative work.

When it did become law, the Directive affected the PMAS in two direct ways as anticipated – one allowed it to invest directly overseas rather than doing so through unit trusts and investment trusts; the PMAS did take advantage of this and now invests directly overseas; the second was to subject the PMAS, with effect from 31st December 1988, to an annual actuarial valuation. In its early days, the PMAS had been subjected to actuarial valuations every five years, later being reduced to three and now down to one yearly intervals. This was costly in both time and effort, one effect of which was a resultant amendment to computer programs. There would also be a wider analysis of premium rates, bonuses and investment performances, all resulting from problems experienced by two large life assurance companies, combined with the threat of AIDS. On the positive side it would permit an extension of the Society's powers, partly due to a removal of restrictions upon its investment powers.

A study of consultative papers received from the Registry of Friendly Societies suggested that the PMAS could make application to be authorised under the EC Life Directive, and this could be effective from January 1988.

Another form of member protection came in the Friendly Societies Policyholders' Protection Scheme and after studying the effects of this, the PMAS decided to make application for membership and to amend its own rules accordingly.

Similar provisions had been introduced for insurance companies by the Policyholders Protection Act of 1975 but at that time they did not extend to friendly societies. With the passing of the Financial Services Act of 1986, however, a comparative scheme was to be introduced for friendly societies; its purpose was the wide protection of policyholders. Administration of the new Protection Scheme would be achieved through a company to be established by The Association of Registered Friendly Societies, and in order to benefit from the scheme, the PMAS would have to nominate a person (such as its Secretary or Manager) who would become a member of the Association and thus gain from its benefits. The PMAS felt that becoming a member of this new scheme would be beneficial.

Just as the new team of executives was establishing itself, Mr Clive Hicks, the Society's Chief Underwriter, died unexpectedly. He had suffered a dislocated hip while playing table tennis but complications set in and he died in hospital on 6th July 1987, having joined the PMAS in August 1978. Following his death, the General Manager commissioned a 'Clive Hicks Cup' to be presented each year at the Society's annual Dinner Dance. It was to be awarded to the member of staff who had, over a period, made a significant contribution to the welfare of fellow members of staff. The cup was inscribed 'Thank God for those who care', the final line of a poem written by Clive a few days before his death.

High drama came to the PMAS in October 1987 with the worldwide collapse in stockmarkets, a financial disaster which has become known as Black Monday. Within two or three days, the world's stockmarkets lost around 20% of their value and millions of pounds were wiped off the value of shares. There was panic among private citizens as well as institutions whose income and security depended upon those shares, and it was a most worrying time for those in charge of PMAS investments.

If there was any solace, it was that the market had been priced too high since Big Bang, the deregulation of a year earlier, but the fall in value was alarming. There is no doubt it was exaggerated by the new computer dealing systems which worked so swiftly, but the PMAS did not submit to panic selling. It sat tight and by that year end, the markets began to recover. Nonetheless, there was extreme caution and some fear of a recession, but the broad spread of the PMAS investments held firm. Its members were not adversely affected by short-term problems of the stockmarket.

At this time, the police service itself was undergoing changes, both internally due to reorganisation and through having to cope with new legislation, in particular the effects of PACE, the Police and Criminal Evidence Act of 1984. This had greatly altered many of its standard procedures so far as arrests, interrogations and detentions were concerned.

Schemes like Neighbourhood Watch were becoming widespread and popular, but new problems like the disease known as AIDS (Acquired Immune Deficiency Syndrome) were also having an effect. There were practical problems for officers who had to arrest or deal with sufferers and hold them in custody; most certainly, there was a risk to the arresting officers' health and to others who had to deal with AIDS sufferers.

From the aspect of the life assurance business, the onset of AIDS had also become a matter of great concern. There was the sensitive matter of potential members having to answer very personal medical questions on application forms – and it was pointed out that some sufferers from AIDS might not even know they had the disease. Should all applicants therefore be subject to an AIDS test? Or was that a gross intrusion into their privacy? Bearing in mind all aspects of this disease, the entire life assurance industry decided to tighten its procedures to identify those at risk. It was pointed out that the additional mortality risk of those affected by AIDS was very high and could have a markedly adverse effect upon funds.

It was decided that proposal forms should contain a specific AIDS question in addition to the usual health information, and there would be a supplementary questionnaire for the proposer's medical attendant to complete. Blood tests were recommended if the applicant was a known or suspected homosexual male, and if he was a single person proposing a life assurance of £250,000 or above.

If these were the recommendations of the life assurance industry, it was left to individual companies and societies to determine their own approach to this matter. The PMAS recognised that it was an expert in the very specialised market in which it dealt and so far as some of its policies were concerned, the risks were minimal. Nonetheless, it did make provision for unforeseen AIDS problems by creating a special AIDS Reserve Fund of £1 million, later reduced to £800,000.

Perhaps the Society was mindful of similar problems which had beset the PMAA some 75 years earlier?

Policies with low risk attached included the 10-year Money-spinner, the endowment policies and capital growth bond contracts. In the case of the other business conducted by the PMAS, where the sums assured were much higher, it was felt that efforts should be made to identify any likely 'at risk' cases. If the PMAS failed to do this, then substantial claims might be made against it and so it would become vulnerable. It was felt that AIDS had received such wide publicity that applicants for life assurance would not be surprised or antagonistic if relevant questions appeared on their proposal forms. It was therefore decided to include questions about AIDS and other sexually transmitted diseases on the proposal forms for the following policies:

Commutation Protection
POLICE 4000
Convertible Option Policy
Low Cost Endowment
Mortgage Protection

This problem having been settled, the question of admission to the PMAS of civilian employees within the police service was again resurrected. Because this request was regularly repeated, (even if it was done in recognition that the turn-over of civilian staff was higher than that of police officers), it was decided to refer the matter to the Standing Sub-Committee of the Committee of Management for further detailed consideration to be made.

It was a matter which would continue to be debated in the future and so a firm effort had to be made to settle the issue. In the wide ranging discussions which ensued, the different classes of employee within the police service were highlighted. Throughout the country, there was a wide variation – some were civil servants, some were employed by local authorities and some were employed by private contractors. Deduction of premiums from their pay could present difficulties along with a very high turn-over of civilian staff, many leaving police employment after a comparatively short period. As things stood, the exclusive nature of the PMAS provided it with great strength; that strength and exclusivity had created its enormous success.

It was felt that nothing should be done to take control of the Society out of police hands. At the end of a long discussion, it was decided that membership of the PMAS should continue to be restricted to members of the police service and their spouses, as it was at that time.

Nonetheless, it was felt that special consideration should be given to the permanent staff at Alexandra House who were directly employed by the PMAS.

Until now, no member of that staff, not even the person holding the highest office, i.e. the Manager & Secretary, was permitted to join the Society they helped to manage so well. It was felt that such permanent staff members were indeed part of the nationwide 'PMAS family' and as such should be allowed to become members.

It seemed only right that their life assurance needs were catered for by their own Society rather than any other commercial company. Deductions of premiums from pay would present no problems. It was therefore agreed by the Committee of Management that membership should be extended to the Society's permanent staff at Alexandra House. The terms would be the same as for police officers and this change would, of course, require a change in the existing rules.

Another area under scrutiny was the role of Chairman of the Management Committee. It was recognised that the increasingly complex world of life assurance and its associated matters had placed an enormous burden on the PMAS as a whole; its senior personnel were now expected to shoulder even greater burdens of responsibility, and the demands on the Chairman had also significantly increased. It was therefore decided that a review of the entire organisation of the PMAS, its management strategy and its work would be conducted, and that the duties of the Chairman of the Management Committee would also be subjected to close examination.

Mr Furber, the incumbent Chairman, was in full agreement with this and he emphasised that he was concerned about the future of the Society rather than his own personal position. Throughout its 66 years, the Society had had only five Chairmen of its Management Committee, Mr Furber being the fifth. The fourth, the popular James Wright, retired in 1980 after a long illness, having been Chairman for almost eleven years. It had always been held by a serving and then retired senior police officer on an entirely voluntary basis, just as all Authorised Officers, the President and the Vice Presidents had all served during their full time occupation. Among the problems which faced the PMAS, especially through an increasingly civilianised police service, were the following:

Where could the Society most appropriately:

(a) recruit future members of the Committee of Management?

(b) find a future Chairman with suitable experience?

(c) give suitable experience to those taking up office?

It also addressed the question as to whether it was right and proper for the highly demanding office of Chairman to be held under the present arrangements, i.e. voluntarily and unpaid. Its many responsibilities, including the administration of massive funds held in trust for others, demanded exceptional qualities and was comparable with that of a non-executive chairman of a very successful commercial company.

Following discussions at the Home Office between the Society's President, Mr R.S. (later Sir Richard) Barratt, Mr Furber and Mr Sharpe, the Committee of Management determined that the responsibilities of the Chairman would be reviewed at length, that a suitable method of appointing future chairmen be determined and that consideration would be given to the payment of an honorarium to the Chairman, unless, of course, the post was held by a serving police officer.

One result of the Financial Services Act of 1986 was to affect Authorised Officers – there was a total of some 600 throughout Britain, comprising Force and Divisional Authorised Officers. In 1988, they were formally appointed as company representatives in order to comply with the provisions of that statute, although in the case of the PMAS they retained the name of Authorised Officer and continued to work for no remuneration or commission.

During 1988, the PMAS faced many other changes – its own staff pension scheme had to be revised to meet statutory demands because new employees were free to arrange their own personal pension plans, existing staff members could opt out of the occupational scheme to arrange personal plans, there were more changes to the Life Assurance Premium Relief (LAPR) which entailed contacting every holder of a policy issued before 14th March 1984 to explain the changes (a reduction from 15% to 12.5% with the resultant changes to premiums) and a reform of life assurance taxation which demanded further additional administrative effort.

At a meeting of the Committee of Management in October 1988, Mr Furber, the Chairman, reported that the PMAS was coping with unprecedented changes brought about by new financial regulations which affected all friendly societies and life assurance companies, and he complimented the staff at Alexandra House. They had met the changes with determination, enthusiasm and a sense of challenge, but those changes and the impact made by them, would continue to place heavy demands upon the staff. Their level of commitment won the highest praise from everyone associated with the PMAS.

It was in 1988 that approval was given for work to commence on the new extension at Alexandra House – the need for this had long been accepted and it was with some sense of relief that in August 1988 the contractors moved in to begin their work. The Building Sub-Committee overseeing this project comprised Mr J.R. Furber, Mr T.C. Hancock, an elected member of the Committee from the West Midlands, and Mr Sharpe. The appointed architect was Mr P. E. Brownhill, Dip. Arch. RIBA, of the Duval Brownhill Partnership, a respected local architect who had architectural responsibility for the Cathedral Close of Lichfield; the building contractor was another local firm, Friary Construction.

Work progresses on the new extension to Alexandra House

As the building work progressed, so the changes to the Society intensified. Following the merger of Duncan C. Fraser, the Society's consulting actuaries, with an American firm called William M. Mercer-MPA to become Mercer Fraser, Mr D.E.A. Sanders, BSc, FIA, announced his resignation from this enlarged firm. Sadly, this meant he had to sever his links with the PMAS.

Although David Sanders had been the Society's actuary for only a short time, he had assisted the previous actuary, Muir McKelvey, for many years. His commitment to the PMAS had always exceeded that expected of a normal commercial/professional relationship and his enthusiasm would be greatly missed. This was yet another example of the changing environment in which the Society now operated.

In the short term, the PMAS maintained its relationship with Mercer Fraser as the overall review of the management structure progressed.

Special consideration was being given to the composition, role and responsibilities of the Society's Investment Committee. The old style sub-committee had served the PMAS with distinction since 1961, but the consulting actuary, bank manager and auditor now had other pressing demands upon their time and there was a call for greater arms-length independence in the new financial environment.

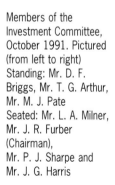

Members of the Investment Committee, October 1991. Pictured (from left to right) Standing: Mr. D. F. Briggs, Mr. T. G. Arthur, Mr. M. J. Pate Seated: Mr. L. A. Milner, Mr. J. R. Furber (Chairman), Mr. P. J. Sharpe and Mr. J. G. Harris

The search began for independent non-executive directors of the highest calibre. They were required to serve on the Investment Committee and also to sit on the full Committee of Management. The first appointment was Mr Leslie A. Milner, FCA. He had recently retired as Finance Director of McKechnie, a British industrial company with world-wide interests. He was well versed in dealing with the City and his appointment was to prove a great success.

A few months later, a second independent non-executive director was appointed. He was Mr John G. Harris, FCA, who headed his own accountancy firm. Previously, he had been a much respected managing partner of Arthur Young, the Society's auditors, so he brought to the PMAS his professional expertise coupled with a long-standing knowledge of the Society.

Meanwhile, the Manager, Mr Sharpe, was talking with investment professionals and stockbrokers, with the aim of appointing top-class fund managers so that, with the Investment Committee and the professional staff at Alexandra House, the Society would have an investment team of the highest quality. Final recommendations were submitted and approved by the Committee of Management in January 1989.

The Investment Committee maintained a general overview of investment matters, the approval of policy and transactions since the previous meeting, and of performance and progress.

The duties of the Investment Department, such a crucial one to the Society, were extensive and included:

(a) maintenance and compilation of investment records
(b) advising on capital gains tax liabilities and highlighting the effect of tax upon proposed investment transactions
(c) producing outflow and inflow projections
(d) investment of cash
(e) collation of equity research and production of specific recommendations

The cover of a PMAS video

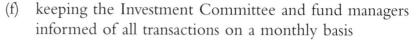

(f) keeping the Investment Committee and fund managers informed of all transactions on a monthly basis

(g) dealing, except in areas subject to discretionary investment by external fund managers

(h) measurement of performance.

The Investment Department would receive external fund advice within clearly defined areas, and the Society's actuary would also maintain an advisory role. Day-to-day management of the Investment Fund would be the responsibility of the internal and external fund managers.

At a more localised level, the PMAS decided to register for Value Added Tax (VAT) with HM Customs and Excise, a means by which it would benefit through its investment properties; the Society's Life Vice President, Mr Albert (Bert) Treves celebrated his 80th birthday and his 50th year of association with the PMAS, and as a means of distributing its message, the PMAS produced a

Peter McCann of BBC's 'Tomorrow's World' at work on a PMAS promotional video

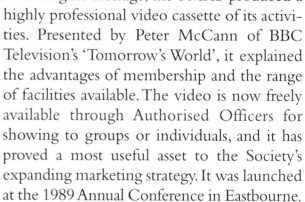

highly professional video cassette of its activities. Presented by Peter McCann of BBC Television's 'Tomorrow's World', it explained the advantages of membership and the range of facilities available. The video is now freely available through Authorised Officers for showing to groups or individuals, and it has proved a most useful asset to the Society's expanding marketing strategy. It was launched at the 1989 Annual Conference in Eastbourne.

At the same conference, Mr J. R. Furber received a well deserved honour – he was elected a Life Vice President and the award was made by the President, Sir Richard Barratt.

He took the opportunity to comment on Mr Furber's unquestionable loyalty, devotion and dedication to the Society, and described him as a man of great sincerity, integrity and industry. Sir Richard went on to say that he had had a long personal association with Mr Furber; they had served together in the Cheshire Constabulary in the 1950s and Mr Furber had been a member of the Management Committee of the PMAS for many years. He had progressed to become a very distinguished Chairman. The Committee of Management had agreed that his outstanding service should be recognised in a fitting and special manner. Sir Richard said that it was his honour to propose that the PMAS bestow upon Mr Furber the highest accolade of a Life Vice Presidency. Mr Treves was delighted to second the motion which would give Mr Furber the rank which Mr Treves was himself exceedingly proud to hold.

Mr Furber replied that he felt honoured to be elected a Life Vice President of the Society, an accolade which, so far as he was aware, had been bestowed upon only four other members of the Society. He added that he was deeply privileged to be associated with them, in particular with the sole surviving Life Vice President, Mr Bert Treves. It was a proud moment which he would always treasure.

Meanwhile, the review of the management structure was proceeding, the new Head Office extension was nearing completion and the computer system was in need of upgrading.

The Society was continuing its practice of visiting forces and training centres with a policy of quickly responding to any request to address a group of officers, anywhere within the British Isles at any time. The Society's speakers attended courses in public speaking at Alexandra House, and tried to visit every force at least once a year, including those in the Channel Isles, the Isle of Man and Northern Ireland. The whole range of police personnel, from recruits to those attending pre-retirement courses, was addressed by the PMAS team of speakers.

In addition, it continued with its Book Prize for students at training centres, as well as support for the annual Snowdonia

HRH The Prince of Wales presenting the PMAS Book Prize at a Police Training Centre, on the occasion of an annual ceremonial parade

Seven mountain trial, now a firmly established event.

In these varied ways, Head Office works hard to establish and maintain contact with police officers. Much of this work is done through the Authorised Officers who distribute the PMAS range of literature such as leaflets and posters, or who place on display the various visual aids, but the Society does also maintain a very close and friendly contact with police organisations such as the Police Federation, the Superintendents' Association, ACPO, NARPO, the District Training Centres, the Central Planning Unit and police magazines, whether at national or force level. Regular local seminars are also held when Authorised Officers at force or divisional level get together to exchange ideas and views with PMAS personnel.

Furthermore, any police officer can call at Alexandra House or telephone the staff, and always be sure of a friendly reception. The Society prides itself on the accessibility of its staff – instant communication is regarded as essential if the needs of police officers are to be effectively and efficiently dealt with. 24-hour answering phones, a freepost facility and facsimile machines have all been introduced to respond to the challenge, and members of the PMAS staff have been trained to cope with professional and technical enquiries, both in written and spoken forms, from every part of the United Kingdom. The interests of the consumer always come first and the PMAS quite justifiably prides itself on the manner in which it cares for its clients.

It is perhaps wise at this point to mention the atmosphere of the Society's Annual Conference. Without doubt, this is the high point of the year when police officers may attend to meet and talk with PMAS officers and staff in a very informal and friendly way.

It has been the practice of the PMAS, right from its foundation, to hold its conferences at different venues so that police officers from all parts of the UK have the opportunity to attend and meet the staff. There is no doubt that the Conference does motivate Authorised Officers who meet one another to discuss problems and methods of operation, and it is the Society's keystone to the dissemination of up-to-date information and to increasing the rapport between the Society, the authorised officers and all police personnel.

Another aspect of the Society's involvement with outside organisations and personnel is the manner in which Head Office staff take an active part in local matters. One example is their participation in events in Lichfield and district, including sporting and cultural activities, while the PMAS has actively supported the Restoration Appeal for Lichfield Cathedral. As a major employer within the City, this was regarded as an important aspect of relations with the local people. The facilities at Alexandra House have helped to create a team spirit among the staff and their families. Social functions can be held at Alexandra House or elsewhere, there are outings to the theatre or to dinner/dances, sporting events and other activities which involve the staff and their families. Some involve employees from other organisations in the area, and this constant air of friendliness is regarded as a highly important feature of the work of the PMAS.

PMAS Head Office staff at leisure

The Society's Force Liaison Officer, Nigel Capewell, who represented Great Britain in the World and European Cycling Championships for the disabled

The PMAS team before a raft race

The PMAS cricket team

Joanne Baskerville — winner of the Lichfield Pancake Race 1990

By the end of 1989, the office extension had been completed and the building had been furnished and decorated. Staff were able to move into their new accommodation and an official opening ceremony was planned for the following spring, with the Right Honourable The Viscount Whitelaw, a former Deputy Prime Minister and Home Secretary, as guest of honour.

Following extensive restructuring of the managerial functions and procedures at Alexandra House, a recommendation from the Manager was approved that independent management consultants be called in to conduct a management audit.

They were asked to report accordingly. Their comprehensive report, which was received in May 1989, included a recommendation that a financial executive should be appointed and that the titles of the executives should be changed to convey the nature and scope of their current responsibilities.

As a result, the executive titles of the following personnel were changed to that which appears below:

Mr P. J. Sharpe, FCII – General Manager
Mr M. J. Kilgallen, FCII – Assistant General Manager – Marketing
Mr M. J. Pate, FCII – Assistant General Manager – Technical
Mr I.V. Dempster, BA – Assistant General Manager – Operations
Mr A.P. Hunter, BSc, ACA – Assistant General Manager – Resources

This management audit is now conducted annually.

One of the first challenges to confront the new team was the effect of a Government Green Paper, published at the beginning of 1990, which called for a new framework for Friendly Societies. The foreword was written by Mr John Major, the then Chancellor of the Exchequer and later Prime Minister. He commented,

"The traditional values on which friendly societies are based may seem to some people to be out of step with the current highly competitive financial services market. But the Government believes they are values which are worth protecting and fostering. Mutuality and competition can go hand in hand.

The Building Sub-Committee placing a time capsule in the extension to Alexandra House. (From left to right) Mr. P. J. Sharpe, Mr. T. C. Hancock and Mr. J. R. Furber

The Government hopes the proposals in this Green Paper will provide the societies with firmer footing in the modern world and secure the future of the friendly societies into the next century."

The Government had recognised that some friendly societies had been restricted by the legislation which governed them, and there had been a sympathetic response from HM Treasury to the societies' requests for wider powers. For example, commercial life assurance companies could provide other services by establishing subsidiary companies, but this facility was not available to friendly societies. Because they were unincorporated bodies, they could not establish subsidiary companies. If a friendly society became an insurance company in order to widen its scope, then it would lose its special identity. To overcome this, the Green Paper proposed that the new legislation should enable friendly societies to convert to corporate status which in turn would allow them to retain their special identity. A friendly society could then, if it wished, establish subsidiary companies to provide, *inter alia,* personal equity plans, unit trusts and introduce general insurance, or it could adopt wider powers to provide life assurance, such as allowing an unmarried couple who were buying a house together to insure each other's lives.

It was emphasised, however, that friendly societies should not be allowed to expand their other interests to such an extent that they lost sight of their prime objectives, and it was suggested that the Registry of Friendly Societies remained as a supervisory authority.

Another suggestion was that friendly societies be required to join a compensatory scheme established by the Policyholders' Protection Act of 1975, and an ombudsman scheme. There were further proposals about the composition of the Committees of Management and the management of funds but the PMAS was already operating such a system of safeguards.

In examining the Government's proposals, the PMAS expressed the view that it would be reassuring to know that it would be possible for it to move into other areas of finance should its members desire it, and it had no objections to the resultant tightening of any necessary regulations.

In the early months of 1990, following the welcome news that Lord Whitelaw had accepted an invitation from the President, Sir Richard Barratt, to open the extension to Alexandra House, the necessary preparations were put into action for what was to be a memorable day in the Society's history.

Among the other matters relating to the work of the Society was the recognition that the PMAS needed the services of committed young professionals.

It must recruit young people with management potential and it was agreed that a programme of training and career development should be implemented. Many clerically based jobs were now computerised and, with the continuing and increasing flow of new legislation plus constant change, it was vital that the very best staff be recruited; it was also necessary that they remain with the PMAS and that their work be seen as a worthwhile career.

A further product of the review of management strategy came to fruition during 1990 with the publication of detailed amendments to the terms of reference for the Committee of Management, the duties and method of appointment of its Chairman and related matters such as appointing a Deputy Chairman, other committees and sub-committees, non-executive directors and specifications of the duties of the General Manager, and his Assistant General Managers.

It was during 1990 that an idea was floated for the implementation of another new type of policy. Research had shown that some police officers had been tempted by contracts with very low premiums, even if they did offer very low returns or smaller benefits. The Society could produce a policy of this kind, although potential members would have to be told that it was a special low-cost endowment scheme with a lower return. The policy would not compete with any of the PMAS existing schemes.

Committee of Management and officers in the boardroom prior to their meeting in March, 1991.
(From left to right) Standing: Mr. A. P. Hunter, Mr. I. V. Dempster, Mr. C. Henderson, Miss G. Miles
(later Mrs. Maxwell), Mr. M. G. Bowd, Mr. B. Williams, Mr. G. E. Livingston, Mr. M. J. Foster,
Mr. D. W. Perkins, Mr. L. A. Milner, Mr. J. G. Harris, Mr. D. S. Parmee, Mr. M. J. Kilgallen
Seated: Mr. D. J. Plester, Mr. W. R. Parry, Mr. A. E. Treves, Mr. J. R. Furber (Chairman),
Mr. C. H. Kelly (CC, Staffordshire), Mr. P. J. Sharpe, Mr. N. G. Pocknell

Detailed plans for this would be considered and, if agreeable, it would be launched early in 1991, probably around the time of the Annual Conference.

On Tuesday 20th March 1990, the new extension to Alexandra House was officially opened by the Right Honourable Viscount Whitelaw, CH, MC, DL, almost 20 years to the day after Head Office had been formally opened by HRH Princess Alexandra. It was a happy occasion at which Lord Whitelaw unveiled a plaque which can now be seen within the building.

Right Lord Whitelaw opens the extension to Alexandra House on 20th March, 1990 (from left to right) Mr. P. J. Sharpe (General Manager), Mr. J. R. Furber (Chairman) and Sir Richard Barratt (President), with Lord Whitelaw after the opening ceremony

Centre left Talking to Mr. C. H. Kelly (CC, Staffordshire) and Sir Stanley Bailey (CC, Northumbria), both Vice Presidents

Centre right Meeting Authorised Officers. (From left to right) Mr. M. Baumber (Warwickshire), Miss P. Low (Avon & Somerset), Mr. D. W. Franklin (Thames Valley), Mr. M. J. Farthing (Durham), Mr. H. J. Graham (Suffolk) and Mr. M. H. Farr (Northamptonshire)

Bottom The top table at luncheon prior to the opening ceremony. (From left to right) Mr. J. R. Furber, Lady Barratt, Lord Whitelaw, Sir Richard Barratt, Mrs. Furber, Mr. C. H. Kelly and Mrs. Kelly

Bottom Left Cover of commemorative edition of 'Lifeline'

At the 1990 Annual General Meeting in Bowness-on-Windermere, Sir Richard Barratt retired as the Society's President. He was succeeded by Sir John Woodcock, HM Chief Inspector of Constabulary for England and Wales.

It was during 1990 that the Head Office computer equipment was upgraded by the installation of a VAX 4000 system, to be followed in 1991 with the purchase of personal computers to replace existing word processors.

And, in spite of all the unproductive administrative work involved with LAUTRO and new legislation during the preceding months, the total funds of the PMAS soared to £350 million in 1990, and its total annual income rose to a staggering £58 million, more than £36 million of which arose from premiums. This had been done in the face of increasing competition from commercial companies but without yielding to their highly pressurised sales methods. During the same period, the PMAS also paid out more than £33.5 million in benefits, much of it to members whose policies had matured.

Nonetheless, the PMAS was not complacent and realised that there were still many police officers who were not members and this prompted it to launch yet another policy. This was the Minimum Low Cost Endowment Policy which had been discussed during 1990; it was introduced to the police service during the Annual Conference of 1991 at Harrogate. One disturbing factor had emerged during the research which led to the inception of this new policy – some officers had been persuaded by commercial insurance companies to surrender their policies so that they could take out new contracts with those commercial companies. Surrenders of this kind were rarely in the interest of the members concerned. It was hoped that the introduction of a special low cost policy would halt that trend.

At the end of 1990, the Society said "Goodbye" to Mr Ralph Long on his retirement after serving on the staff since 1963. He was especially known for his visits to training centres, liaison work with the Police Federation at whose conferences he was a regular attender, and for his role as Chairman of the staff PMAS Sports and Social Association. It was at this time that the Society appointed its first Personnel Manager, Miss Margaret Dalton, MIPM.

The 1991 Conference at Harrogate was momentous. The Delegate Council approved a change of rule regarding election to the Committee of Management.

The Consulting Actuary confirmed an increase in the Society's bonus rates, and the Committee of Management approved a third non-executive director to sit on the Investment Committee and the Committee of Management. He was Mr Terry G. Arthur, BSc, FIA. Mr Arthur, an actuary who specialised in institutional investment, had previously been connected with the PMAS when he worked for Duncan C. Fraser with Muir McKelvey prior to setting up his own firm.

With David Parmee, BSc, FIA, of Bacon & Woodrow, being confirmed as the Society's Consulting Actuary, there was now a clear distinction between those professional associates who worked for the Society on a day-to-day basis, and those who sat as independent non-executive directors on the Committee of Management.

This guarded against any possible conflict of interest and accorded with accepted modern commercial practice. Nevertheless, the PMAS maintained its long-standing links with the past. Lloyds Bank was still the Society's banker after over 70 years and Ernst & Young, the auditors, still maintained their link through Newton and Co and Arthur Young after successive mergers.

At the 1991 Harrogate Conference, two new awards were introduced. They were the Society's Award of Merit and the President's Certificate of Commendation.

It was announced that the first recipient of the Award of Merit, which was to be strictly limited to emphasise the special status of the award, was to be made to Mr Bert Treves, the Society's senior Life Vice President who had then been connected with the PMAS for some 50 years.

The President's Certificate of Commendation was to enable the Society to give special recognition to those Authorised Officers who had given highly commendable service over a substantial period of time.

The climax of that Conference came with the presentation to the Society of its Armorial Bearings. During 1990, the Chairman had expressed a view that it was now appropriate for the Society to secure its own Grant of Arms. Enquiries were launched in an attempt to determine the feasibility of this and advice was sought from experts in heraldry and from the College of Arms. It was widely accepted that the Society's image would be considerably enhanced by the grant of its own armorial bearings and so steps were taken to facilitate the grant. The Arms were presented by Sir John Woodcock to the Chairman, Mr Furber, who accepted them on behalf of the Society. They symbolically represent the Society's involvement with both the police service and assurance, the Society's origins in Birmingham and its present home in Lichfield. The motto is 'Servire et servare' – to serve and protect. The armorial bearings are reproduced on the cover of this book and upon items of PMAS stationery.

Annual Conference, Harrogate, 1991. Presentation of armorial bearings by the President, Sir John Woodcock, to the Chairman, Mr. John Furber, who accepted them on behalf of the Society. The arms are now on display at Alexandra House

As the Police Mutual moved into the 1990s and towards the 21st century, the General Manager's report to the meeting of the Management Committee on 9th October 1991, which was attended by the President, Sir John Woodcock, gave an interesting insight into the work of the Society and its connection with the police service. It was reported that the level of new business was running at record levels and the market value of total assets had exceeded £400 million for the first time. Tributes were paid to the outstanding commitment of the Society's Authorised Officers and the marketing team at Head Office.

The first awards of the President's Certificate of Commendation were made to Mr W. R. Parry, LLB, (Hampshire), Mr D. J. Plester (South Yorkshire) and Mr N.G. Pocknell (Gwent). In addition to being senior members of the Committee of Management, they had all been, for a number of years, most effective Authorised Officers in their particular forces.

An extensive visiting programme had been undertaken by members of the PMAS executive and senior staff, and this included attendance at conferences of ACPO, the Police Superintendents' Association and the Police Federation; there were also visits to police training centres, the Central Planning Unit, force pre-retirement courses and individual forces, including the Royal Ulster Constabulary.

The Committee agreed to a request from the Director of the Central Planning Unit to meet the cost of a revised 'Police Powers and Definitions' booklet which was to include a list entitled '20 Points to Prove' relating to the commission of the most common crimes. This booklet includes promotional material from the PMAS and is to be distributed to some 120,000 serving officers through ACPO.

Another factor which affected the Society was the pending enactment of the Friendly Societies Bill which received Royal Assent in March 1992. In the March Budget of 1991, the Government had indicated its wish to promote savings for the benefit of

The Society owns
several prestigious
investment properties
throughout Britain.
These photographs
show a small selection

203

children by introducing, in the Finance Act of 1991, changes to the rules applicable to friendly societies.

Steps to recruit a new member to the executive and to appoint a Chief Accountant at Head Office were approved. Further progress by Head Office staff in their professional examinations had increased the depth of experience available to the PMAS, and the Committee discussed further ways of providing cover and continuity on the Committee itself.

The historic relationship between the PMAS and Staffordshire Police was endorsed by the decision of the Committee to participate in the 150th Anniversary Celebrations of Staffordshire Police in 1992. This included a concert by the National Police Orchestra in Lichfield Cathedral and hosting a reception at Alexandra House. Mr Charles Kelly, the Chief Constable of Staffordshire and a Vice President of the Society, commented that it was most appropriate that the PMAS should be involved in those celebrations as the two organisations were intertwined.

Seventy years have passed since the foundation of the PMAS in 1922 and it has been an astonishing success story in which the Society has progressed from an overdraft of £2,000 to one with assets of more than £400 million. By the end of 1991, some 40,000 new policies had been issued in just one year and the Society's annual income was around £84 million, money which continues to be invested for the benefit of police officers throughout Britain. It is a tremendous story and an achievement of which every police officer can be rightly proud. After all, the PMAS is their very own Society.

But it is a story which is far from finished. For one thing, we still do not know the identity of the mysterious police writer, 'Verdad' whose idea started the whole story!

SELECTED CONTRIBUTIONS

In assembling information for inclusion in this book, we approached many people who were, or who had been, associated with the PMAS over the years. Most of their memories and reminiscences are included within the text but it was felt that some contributions were worthy of reproduction in their entirety.

One came from Sir George Terry, CBE, QPM, DL, a former Chief Constable of Pembrokeshire, East Sussex, Lincolnshire and Sussex, and a Vice President of the Society. He comments on his involvement with the PMAS from his first day in the Force.

"On my very first day on the beat as a Constable in the Birmingham City Force, I was instructed to report to the Station Sergeant at Ladywood Road Police Station before going on patrol. Sergeant Prince was also the 'B' Divisional Representative of the PMAS. He gave me an envelope addressed to Mr John Hadley, the then Manager of the Society at its office in Greenfield Crescent, Edgbaston, which was on my beat, with the firm instruction, "Don't lose it, laddie."

I didn't, and above all else I will always remember the warmth of greeting from John when I handed over the envelope, and his good wishes for a successful career in the service.

Little did I think then that John's wishes would be fulfilled and that I would sit with others who had done much more for the Society around the boardroom table in Alexandra House, some forty years later as President of ACPO.

We have always been blessed with someone in the Chair who, above all else, has been a gentleman and a very shrewd person, and they have all been so kind by making everyone feel that they counted.

I have already mentioned John Hadley as the Manager and now, through the present time with Peter Sharpe, the Society seems to have been blessed with their fairness, their friendliness and most of all, their efficiency. There must be a 'mould' somewhere at the Society's HQ from which they emerge – and long may that remain!

The Society, through its Chairman, Officers and *all* the staff, sets an example as to how things should be done with a really true spirit. In this day and age when 'dog eats dog' so readily, the Society stands for value for money and a true Christian attitude of helpfulness and efficiency, and the absence of bureaucracy."

A warm welcome to
Alexandra House

THE AUTHORISED OFFICER

From the very beginning, the PMAS has depended upon a network of volunteers known as Authorised Officers. They comprise the broadest possible spectrum of serving police officers – some chief constables, their deputies and assistants have served as Authorised Officers even while holding those top ranks, just as others have been recruited from sergeants, constables and even cadets, both men and women. Some policemen have acted as authorised officers throughout their career and some have held every rank in the service. Some of the best known officers in the history of the police force have acted as authorised officers at some stage of their service. In addition, the range of authorised officers has included policemen and women working both operationally and in police administration.

Beyond the confines of Alexandra House, the PMAS Head Office in Lichfield, this very representative and very important body of volunteers forms the Society's entire external organisation throughout Great Britain and Northern Ireland. This role has been undertaken by Authorised Officers from the first days of the Society and there is no doubt that their work has provided the basis upon which the Society has flourished. The decision to use these volunteers was masterly.

The role of Authorised Officers is to represent the PMAS and they operate within each of the nation's police forces. In the early days, they operated only at force level, because police forces were not so large as their modern counterparts; their geographic areas and the number of serving officers were far smaller than today, although there were many more forces.

When the PMAS was created, there were 260 police forces in

England, Scotland and Wales; those have now been reduced to 43 in England and Wales with eight in Scotland. (This number differs from those currently served by the PMAS because the Society now serves the police forces of some ports, the Ministry of Defence, the Atomic Energy Authority, Jersey, Guernsey, the Isle of Man, British Transport and the Royal Ulster Constabulary.)

The increase in geographical and numerical size of forces due to amalgamations and local authority boundary changes, means that authorised officers now operate at both force and divisional level.

During the most recent series of amalgamations in 1974, some Force Authorised Officers found themselves working with Authorised Officers from other, often smaller, forces which had been absorbed into larger units. It was then that some differences in procedure occurred – some forces, for example, continued to deduct premiums from retired officers' pensions while others did not.

In many cases, it meant a rationalisation of administrative procedures which produced some rancour as smaller forces found themselves mere divisions in larger units, but these difficulties, minor in retrospect, were quickly overcome.

At the time of going to press there are some 600 Authorised Officers throughout the United Kingdom, including those operating on behalf of the police forces of the Atomic Energy Authority, the Ports of London and Liverpool, the Ministry of Defence and British Transport.

The most important aspect of their work is that they are not paid for their services nor do they draw any commission or monetary rewards of any kind. Their services are entirely free and they are recruited by the PMAS as it seeks volunteers for this vital and worthy work. After a short period of training, and with guidance from Head Office always available, they fulfil this role in addition to their normal police duties.

It is the use of Authorised Officers which has given the

PMAS such a unique place both in the development of the police service and within the realms of Friendly Societies.

As far back as 1923, when the first full year of operation was discussed at the Annual General Meeting in Manchester, the Chairman, the then Inspector B.D. Pinkerton of Birmingham City Police, praised their work to loud applause by saying,

"We are indebted to the work done by the Authorised Officers," adding that their contribution had, even within such a short time, been recognised as a major contribution to the Society's already substantial progress.

Through the development of the Society, the role of the Authorised Officers has never been underestimated and today the PMAS continues to emphasise their importance. In its own words, it says, "The importance of the role of the PMAS Authorised Officer, whether at force or divisional level, cannot be overstated." In performing this important function, many Authorised Officers have developed a deep, long term interest in the Society and its affairs.

George Flett, an Authorised Officer, addressing some young recruits to Grampian Police

Some have progressed to become members of its Committee of Management or even Vice Presidents or President. A modern example is Mr John R. Furber, QPM, formerly Assistant Chief Constable of Cheshire and presently a Life Vice President, Chairman of the Delegate Council and Chairman of the Investment Committee. In 1954, he began his association with the PMAS as an Authorised Officer, later working at both Force and Divisional level, and in 1965 was co-opted as a Member of the Committee of Management.

By 1973, he was deputy Chairman, becoming Chairman and also Vice President in 1980 and then a Life Vice President in 1989.

Another Authorised Officer, a sergeant in Lincolnshire, also achieved a great deal – he is now a member of the House of Lords where his knowledge of the police service is invaluable. He rose through the ranks from cadet to become Commandant of the Police College, Chief Constable of Birmingham and later of the West Midlands. He was Sir Philip, later Lord, Knights who became a Vice President of the PMAS and he made history by being the first police officer to be created a peer.

Philip Knights joined Lincolnshire Constabulary in 1937 and rose through the ranks to become Chief Superintendent. He was appointed Assistant Chief Constable of Birmingham in 1959 and then Deputy Commandant of the Police College at Bramshill in 1963. In 1970, he returned to Birmingham as Deputy Chief Constable and two years later became Chief Constable of the Sheffield and Rotherham Constabulary, assuming command of the South Yorkshire Police in the amalgamations of 1974. In 1975, he returned to West Midlands Police as Chief Constable, a post he held until his retirement in 1985. He was knighted in the New Year Honours List of 1980.

Lord Knights has been closely associated with the PMAS throughout his career. He joined the Society whilst a cadet, served as Authorised Officer when he was a sergeant in Lincolnshire and was appointed Vice President in 1975, a post he held until his retirement in 1985.

To honour his achievements and his elevation to the peerage, a reception was held by the Police Mutual Assurance Society at Alexandra House in Lichfield on Wednesday 7th October 1987. Lord Knights, accompanied by Lady Knights, was guest of honour and he was presented with an inscribed crystal bowl by the

Lord Knights following a presentation to him by the President at Alexandra House in honour of his being created a Peer in 1987. Lord Knights, a former PMAS Authorised Officer, had been a Vice President of the Society from 1975 until 1985 when he retired as Chief Constable of West Midlands Police. Pictured are (from left to right) Standing: Mr. J. R. Furber, Lord Knights, Mr. R. S. (later Sir Richard) Barratt, Mr. P. J. Sharpe
Seated: Lady Knights and Mrs. Sharpe

Society's President, Mr R.S. Barratt, HM Chief Inspector of Constabulary for England and Wales.

It was Lord Knights who pointed out that the PMAS was the only organisation within the police service which embraced all ranks.

Yet another young officer, Andrew Meldrum became an Authorised Officer in the 1930s while a constable with the Stirling County Constabulary and later became a member of the General Management Committee between 1966 and 1969 while serving as HM Chief Inspector of Constabulary for Scotland. He was awarded both the CBE and the KPM. He tells a charming story concerning the PMAS.

"I recall an insurance agent – one of a number – approaching me with a view to taking out a policy with his company. When I told him I was already insured with the PMAS and gave him an indication of the premiums and the sums that would be paid on maturity of the policies, he first did not believe me. The trend of conversation led to bluntness in our exchanges which terminated with the agent saying that policemen were not a very good risk anyway!"

Mr Meldrum went on to say that that early experience made him appreciate how good were the terms offered by the PMAS when compared with other insurance companies.

Woman Sergeant Vera Lee of the North Riding Constabulary made history in 1957 when she became the first woman Authorised Officer. She was succeeded by PC P. N. Walker, the author of this book.

Among the authorised officers, there are many fascinating stories – PC J.G. Bentley, BEM of Merseyside was just one of many outstanding Authorised Officers from Merseyside who made such an outstanding contribution to the Society. When he was awarded the BEM in 1979, the citation referred prominently to his work with the PMAS.

Another story dates from 1969, when Superintendent R. Anderson of Blackburn Borough Police retired having been an authorised officer for over 30 years. He had held this appointment through every one of his ranks – and upon his retirement was awarded 5 guineas (£5. 5s. 0d – £5.25) as a token of appreciation from the Society.

In 1953, Frank Barclay, then a detective sergeant in Greenock Borough Police, became Authorised Officer because he was the only PMAS member out of 200 officers in his force! Once appointed, however, he began to spread news of the benefits of PMAS membership and soon had recruited every member of his force from the Chief Constable to the newest recruit – the only force with a 100% membership of the Society.

At first, he collected all the premiums in person from the members but then succeeded in getting them deducted from the officers' pay.

This complements the story of Sergeant T. Gibson of Edinburgh City Police, an Authorised Officer who, in 1975, was a training officer at the Scottish Police College. He attained over £1 million in new sums assured within the space of 12 months. And then by the following year, he increased that sum to over £3 million. If that achievement seemed impressive, then it was learned that in 1978 another Scottish officer, Sergeant Pilkington of Strathclyde who was seconded to the Scottish Police College, had in less than 12 months as an authorised officer generated new PMAS business with sums assured totalling £4,100,000. It says a lot for the canny financial acumen of our Scottish colleagues.

Another innovation from Scotland came in the form of a special conference of Scottish authorised officers. This was held in Pitlochry on 11th November, 1987 and was opened by Mr A. Morrison, CVO, QPM, HM Chief Inspector of Constabulary for Scotland and a Vice President of the Society.

He expressed particular concern at the level of debt being incurred by many younger officers and urged the meeting to help ensure early and proper financial planning for them through the PMAS. He felt this would help to reduce this worrying problem.

Mr Morrison had a long-standing relationship with the Society. He was in charge of operational policing arrangements during the opening of the new Head Office building in Lichfield by HRH Princess Alexandra, and served as a Vice President from May 1984 until May 1989.

Despite travelling from Scotland, he was a regular attender of meetings of the Committee of Management, and his quiet but most effective contribution was recognised by a special presentation on the occasion of the opening by Lord Whitelaw of the extension to Alexandra House.

There is no doubt that many authorised officers have taken immense pride in their voluntary work and there are some impressive records of service. Alex Stenhouse of Dumfries and Galloway served as an authorised officer for more than 39 years but one of the most outstanding is surely Bert Treves of the City of

Bert Treves (centre), a Life Vice President of the PMAS, receiving the Society's first Certificate of Merit, 1991. Pictured with Mr. Treves are (left) the General Manager, Mr. Peter Sharpe and (right) the Chairman, Mr. John Furber

London Police. In 1959 he had the unusual distinction of being made a Freeman of the City of London, but in 1976, was appointed Life Vice President of the PMAS in honour of his 37 years as an authorised officer and in 1992 he was still a Life Vice President of the PMAS, having served the PMAS for more than half a century – 52 years to date! In 1991, he was awarded the Society's first Award of Merit.

In spite of the fact that many Authorised Officers have extended their interest to become key personalities within the national organisation of the PMAS, it is not expected that they should all become experts in insurance matters!

As the work of the PMAS expands and grows more complex, however, so the demands upon these volunteers are increasing.

In basic terms, they perform a promotional function. Their task is to bring to the notice of all police officers the benefits of belonging to a society which provides life assurance through savings and which, in addition, offers a range of other financial benefits and schemes.

These range from family protection plans to house purchase via endowment assurance and lump sum investments. The appropriate literature and professional advice is provided by the PMAS Head Office and it aids the AOs, as they are known, to bring to the notice of police officers the range of benefits available through their very own Society. One of the best methods is for AOs or even officials from Head Office, to speak to police officers on residential courses, either during their initial training or on refresher or specialist courses at the various police training establishments.

The Authorised Officer also fulfils an administrative function. One of the tasks is to ensure that when a member joins the

PMAS, the necessary procedures are implemented to ensure the regular payment of premiums. In this, the AO works closely with the force pay department and authority treasurer. One of the assets of membership is that payment of premiums can, if desired, be deducted from pay. This has not always been the case. Until well after World War II, most police officers received their wages in cash at a weekly pay parade.

They had to report to the muster room at a specified time to collect their pay packets – and even if they had been on leave or on night duty the previous night, they were expected to present themselves on the pay parade. Many had to appear in uniform and to salute the senior officer who handed over the precious packet before marching smartly off to a second table where a sergeant waited.

Here, they would part with voluntary cash deductions for various funds such as the force sports club, welfare fund or benevolent fund. The money would be collected and recorded at that parade and then passed to the treasurer of the relevant organisation. Among the monies collected were the premiums of those officers who had joined the PMAS; the early members paid 'a bob a week' – a shilling (5p) – which was a lot from their meagre wages.

Many paid their weekly shilling in the belief that it would enable them to buy a house upon retirement. That was the dream of many young constables and it was the task of the Authorised Officer to ensure that all those precious shillings were paid to the PMAS, usually through a local bank account.

The change to a more sophisticated system came when police officers were paid by cheque; one important change was that the money was sent to an officer's home address by post, and not to the police station. This marked the effective end of the dreaded pay parades.

This also meant that the deduction of contributions to clubs or societies like the PMAS had to be restructured; some city or county treasurers realised that it would be a simple matter to deduct such funds at source, and pay them direct to the bank account of the relevant clubs or societies. Later, of course, the advent of computers eased this system, but in the days immediately following World War II when hand-written cash ledgers were still being used, this was an innovation.

Even until 1948, police officers did not pay National Insurance contributions and so the deduction of any voluntary funds from their pay was considered a major advancement. As most police officers detested the old pay parades, these simplified and more personal pay schemes were widely welcomed! It was therefore comparatively easy to convince officers of the merits associated with the deduction of funds at source.

It is difficult to be categoric as to which police force was the first to deduct PMAS premiums from officers' pay, but Cheshire in 1946 was among the first, as were Surrey and possibly Hertfordshire. It was the change from 'pay parade' to 'salary by cheque' that gave the Authorised Officer a more formal role within the parent force. Hitherto, he had collected cash from members; now, he entered an official relationship with the city or county treasurer and so became part of the administration of the parent Force. There is little doubt that this change enhanced the role of the Authorised Officer and that it also gave the PMAS a higher profile.

But not every force had an Authorised Officer and, probably due to the clumsiness of the system for collecting premiums on the old fashioned pay parades, information about the benefits of the PMAS was not reaching all officers; indeed, it was not even reaching all police forces. An awareness of these defects occurred to John Hadley in 1949 during his first six months as Assistant Secretary and, during a period of convalescence after a serious illness, he realised that the PMAS would progress only if:

    (a)   it could interest more police officers in its benefits;

    (b)   an Authorised Officer was appointed in every force;

(c)   premiums were deducted from pay.

It can now be appreciated that implementation of those ideals depended heavily upon the Authorised Officers, but, thanks to them and to those Chief Constables who appreciated the incomparable benefits of PMAS membership, the Society began to be appreciated by an increasing number of officers. One Authorised Officer, Jim Fitzsimmons of Cumbria, readily acknowledged the support given to his PMAS work by his Chief Constable, Mr W. Cavey. Whenever Jim made any request connected with his work for the Society, it was always granted by his helpful Chief Constable. The Chief often said, quite sincerely, "I appreciate what you do for the PMAS." Those words meant such a lot.

The co-operation of Chief Constables, police administrations and local authorities in having premiums deducted from pay won the support of the Police Federation and the concept is now well established and very popular.

But in spite of the luxury of having deductions made from pay, however, officers may, if they wish, arrange such payments through their own bank accounts or building societies. A high proportion have opted to have their premiums deducted from their salaries because this is a very simple, effective and efficient way of regular and beneficial saving.

Officers throughout the country know only too well the joy of receiving a substantial cheque upon the maturity of their policies after such a painless method of saving– there are stories of some going on world tours upon their retirement, thanks to the PMAS. The PMAS is grateful for the co-operation received from the treasurers of the participating police authorities in their co-operation with the administration of this valuable facility.

Larger police forces with increased areas and more personnel have placed increasingly heavy demands upon authorised officers at both force and divisional level but their response to every new challenge has been magnificent. In 1988, through the effects of the Financial Services Act of 1986, their role became more formalised and they were all appointed official representatives of the Society. But their voluntary status has not changed.

They remain the backbone of the Society. Generations of members of the Society have cause to be grateful to all Authorised Officers, past, present and future. Their selfless dedication has done, and will continue to do, so much to benefit their colleagues and their colleagues' families throughout the British police service.

Double vision! Twin members of the PMAS, Garry and Steve Parker of Hampshire Constabulary pictured with their Authorised Officer, Superintendent Bill Parry at the Force Training Centre

PRESIDENTS OF THE PMAS

1922 – 1992

It has been customary for the Society to appoint, as its President, one of Her Majesty's Inspectors of Constabulary. When the office of HM Chief Inspector of Constabulary for England and Wales was established in 1963, it then became customary to invite holders of that office to become President. Among the Vice Presidents, it has been customary to include distinguished senior police officers from England, Wales, Scotland and Northern Ireland.

The following is a list of the Society's Presidents:

1922   Sir Leonard Dunning, Bart.

1938   Sir Frank Brook, DSO, MC

1957   Sir William Johnson, CMG, CBE (the first Chief HMI)

1963   Sir Edward Dodd, CBE

1967   Sir Eric St Johnston, CBE

1971   Sir John McKay, CBE, QPM

1973   Sir John Hill, CBE, DFC, QPM

1976   Sir James Haughton, CBE, QPM

1977   Sir Colin Woods, KCVO, CBE

1979   Sir James Crane, CBE

1983   Sir Lawrence Byford, CBE, QPM, LLB

1987   Sir Richard Barratt, CBE, QPM

1990   Sir John Woodcock, CBE, QPM, CBIM

CHAIRMEN OF COMMITTEE

1922 – 1992

In its seventy years, the PMAS has had only five Chairmen of its General Committee, later known as its Committee of Management. They are as follows:

1922 Jan	Mr F. H. Mardlin was appointed Chairman of the then Police Mutual Assurance Association. He remained Chairman when the PMAA became the PMAS in March, 1922. He retired due to ill health.
1922 May	Mr B.D. Pinkerton was appointed Chairman of the Police Mutual Assurance Society. He was Chairman for the following 30 years, retiring in 1952. He died in 1953.
1952	Mr E.S. Drake was appointed Chairman. He retired in 1970, having been Chairman for 17 years. He died in 1973.
1969	Mr J. Wright was appointed Chairman. He retired in 1980 after 11 years in the post. He died in 1987.
1980	Mr J.R. Furber was appointed Chairman. He remains in office.

SECRETARIES AND CHIEF EXECUTIVES

Police Mutual Assurance Association

Mr J. Howe was the last Secretary of the PMAA and continued as Secretary to the newly formed PMAS until its first Annual General Meeting in 1922.

Police Mutual Assurance Society

1922 – 1954	Captain S.A. Wood
1954 – 1975	Mr J.W. Hadley, MBE, FCII
1975 – 1986	Mr A.F. King, OBE, FCII
1986 to date	Mr P.J. Sharpe, FCII

ANNUAL MEETINGS

T he Annual Conference, which is usually held over two days in May, is the single most important event of the Society's year. The formal business includes meetings of standing committees, a meeting of the Delegate Council and, in recent years, a seminar especially designed to consult with delegates and to update them with current developments.

Traditionally, the President takes the opportunity during his address to the Annual General Meeting to comment on current police matters, an item of great interest not only to delegates but particularly to the Society's guests and associates who greatly value their relationship with the police service through the PMAS.

The Conference also provides an opportunity for delegates, officers and professional associates throughout the United Kingdom to meet and discuss matters, and to plan the year ahead. Many lifelong friendships are made at these conferences and the attendance of wives and husbands, who do so much to support those involved in the work of the Society, helps to make this annual gathering a real family occasion.

Each year, over the years, a tremendous amount of work and planning goes into ensuring that the Annual Conference is not just efficiently run, but that it is an enjoyable and memorable occasion for all who attend.

It has always been the custom of the PMAS to hold its annual meetings at different venues throughout the country. In this way, the Society becomes known to an increasing number of potential members.

The following is a list of all the Annual General Meetings. There were no Annual General Meetings between 1940 and

1945, these being suspended due to World War II although the Committee of Management did continue to meet on a regular basis during the war years.

★★★★★

No.

1   1922 – Lesser Colston Hall, Bristol 12th May
2   1923 – Town Hall, Manchester 18th May
3   1924 – Royal Hotel, Plymouth 15th May
4   1925 – Town Hall, Leeds 15th May
5   1926 – Home Office, London 4th June
6   1927 – St Mungo Hall, Glasgow 6th May
7   1928 – The Law Courts, Cardiff 4th May
8   1929 – Town Hall, Great Yarmouth 10th May
9   1930 – City Chambers, Edinburgh 9th May
10 1931 – The Guildhall, Portsmouth 15th May
11 1932 – Home Office, London 20th May
12 1933 – Town Hall, Liverpool 12th May
13 1934 – Police Headquarters, Newcastle 25th May
14 1935 – Royal Pavilion, Brighton 24th May
15 1936 – Council Chamber, Harrogate 19th June
16 1937 – Home Office, London 4th June
17 1938 – Guildhall, Hull 17th June
18 1939 – Town Hall, Bournemouth 9th June

Due to World War II
no Annual Meetings were held between 1940 and 1945

19 1946 – Home Office, Whitehall 31st May
20 1947 – Public Library, Blackpool 27th June
21 1948 – Police Headquarters, Eastbourne 18th June
22 1949 – Town Hall, Llandudno 3rd June
23 1950 – Royal Hotel, Weymouth 9th June

24 1951 – St Nicholas Hotel, Scarborough 22nd June
25 1952 – Grosvenor Hotel, Morecambe 20th June
26 1953 – Park Hotel, Cardiff 12th June
27 1954 – Grosvenor Hotel, Edinburgh 21st May
28 1955 – University Arms Hotel, Cambridge 20th May
29 1956 – Cairn Hydro Hotel, Harrogate 18th May
30 1957 – The Council House, Birmingham 21st June
31 1958 – Grand Hotel, Folkestone 8th May
32 1959 – Grand Hotel, Torquay 8th May
33 1960 – Crown Hotel, Scarborough 12th May
34 1961 – Royal Hotel, Southport 4th May
35 1962 – Ironmongers' Hall, City of London 22nd June
36 1963 – St George's Hotel, Llandudno 16th May
37 1964 – Royal Hotel, Bangor, N. Ireland 13th May
38 1965 – Hotel Dunblane, Dunblane, Perth 12th May
39 1966 – University Arms Hotel, Cambridge 10th May
40 1967 – Cairn Hotel, Harrogate 13th June
41 1968 – Burlington Hotel, Eastbourne 15th May
42 1969 – Grand Atlantic Hotel, Weston-super-Mare 14th May
43 1970 – St Nicholas Hotel, Scarborough 17th June
44 1971 – Savoy Hotel, Blackpool 12th May
45 1972 – Marsham Court Hotel, Bournemouth 10th May
46 1973 – Peebles Hydro Hotel, Peebles 16th May
47 1974 – Imperial Hotel, Llandudno 8th May
48 1975 – Marsham Court Hotel, Bournemouth 7th May
49 1976 – Grand Atlantic Hotel, Weston-super-Mare 19th May
50 1977 – Crown Hotel, Scarborough 18th May
51 1978 – Queen's Hotel, Eastbourne 10th May
52 1979 – Peebles Hydro Hotel, Peebles 16th May
53 1980 – St George's Hotel, Llandudno 7th May
54 1981 – Palace Hotel, Torquay 20th May
55 1982 – Prince of Wales Hotel, Southport 19th May
56 1983 – Palace Court Hotel, Bournemouth 11th May
57 1984 – Peebles Hydro Hotel, Peebles 10th May

58 1985 – Palace Hotel, Torquay 15th May

59 1986 – Hotel Majestic, Harrogate 14th May

60 1987 – Palace Court Hotel, Bournemouth 13th May

61 1988 – Peebles Hydro Hotel, Peebles 11th May

62 1989 – Queen's Hotel, Eastbourne 10th May

63 1990 – Old England Hotel, Bowness-on-Windermere 16th
            May

64 1991 – Hotel Majestic, Harrogate 15th May

65 1992 – Peebles Hydro Hotel, Peebles 13th May

Pictures from the 1992 Annual Conference at Peebles

The PMAS Annual General Meeting was well supported by Chief Constables from Scotland
Standing: (left to right) Sir Stanley Bailey (Vice President), Mr. J. M. Boyd (HM Inspector of Constabulary for Scotland), Dr. I. T. Oliver (CC, Grampian), Mr. J. W. Bowman (CC, Tayside), Mr. L. Sharp (CC, Strathclyde), Mr. W. McD. Moodie (CC, Fife)
Seated: (left to right) Mr. P. J. Sharpe (General Manager), Mr. J. R. Furber (Chairman), Sir John Woodcock (President), Mr. C. Sampson (HM Chief Inspector of Constabulary for Scotland and a Vice President), Sir William Sutherland, CC, Lothian and Borders attended the Official Luncheon

Annual General Meeting, opened by The Rt. Hon.
The Earl of Minto, Convener, Borders Regional Council

225

PMAS HIGHLIGHTS

1922   Mr F. H. Mardlin appointed Chairman of the General Committee
       January – Sir Leonard Dunning appointed President. 31st March – The Police Mutual Assurance Association became the Police Mutual Assurance Society. The Whole Life Fund was closed; new endowment scheme began. May – the first Annual Meeting of the PMAS. Mr J. Murray Laing appointed Consulting Actuary. Mr J. Howe retired as Secretary of the PMAS having been Secretary of the former PMAA. Captain S. A. Wood appointed Secretary of PMAS.
       Mr F. H. Mardlin resigned as Chairman, ill-health.
       Mr B. D. Pinkerton appointed Chairman of General Committee.
1923   Registered office moved to 161 Corporation St, Birmingham.
1929   Weekly premium income first exceeded £1,000.
1931   Year end – Premium income of £80,000; sums assured exceeded £1 million. 23,000 members.
1932   First maturity claims paid out. May – first Special General Meeting.
1934   Bonus paid. Office accommodation extended. Annual income £90,000. Assets reached £500,000.
1936   Year end – Assets exceeded £600,000.
1938   Weekly instalments of £2,140 collected; 3% management costs; income in excess of £100,000. Record number of policies. April – Sir Leonard Dunning retired as President. June – Lt. Col. (later Sir) Frank Brook elected President.

1940   No AGMs due to World War II. No policies accepted from officers of fighting age.

1946   Mr F. A. Smith appointed to Accounts Department. Year End – Assets worth £1,500,000. 36,000 members.

1948   Mr A. E. (Bert) Treves co-opted to General Committee.

1949   Mr J.W. Hadley appointed Assistant Secretary.

1950s   Early in the 1950s, quarterly visits made to District Police Training Centres by Head Office staff to talk to recruits.

1952   Mr B. D. Pinkerton retired as Chairman; appointed Hon. Vice President of the PMAS. Mr E.S. Drake appointed Chairman of General Committee. Death of Mr J. Murray Laing. Appointment of Mr K.J. Britt as Actuary.

1953   Death of Mr B.D. Pinkerton. Year End – Assets over £2,000,000.

1954   Captain S.A. Wood retired; Mr J.W. Hadley appointed Secretary. PMAS Nominees replaced Trustees. Mr A.F. King appointed Assistant Secretary. Registered Office moved to 10 Greenfield Crescent, Edgbaston, Birmingham. 6,801 new policies issued. Year End – Sum assured over £1 million.

1957   Sir Frank Brook retired as President. Sir William Johnson appointed. First woman authorised officer – W/Sgt Vera Lee, North Riding of Yorkshire Constabulary. Amalgamation of Whole Life/Endowment Funds Year End – Assets worth £2,864,000; premium income in excess of £500,000; investment income reached six figures for first time; increase of £371,870 in Endowment Fund; expenses under 3%. 10,013 new policies.

1958   Royal Ulster Constabulary officers admitted as members.

1959   Mr A.E. Treves awarded Freedom of the City of London.

1960   Death of Sir Frank Brook.

1961   Year end – 17,223 new policies; over £5 million in sums assured; over £1 million in premium contributions. Appointment of Mr N.A. Horsley as Deputy Consulting Actuary.

1962   Title of Secretary changed to Manager & Secretary. Retirement of Mr K.J. Britt, appointed Hon. Vice President. Mr N.A. Horsley appointed Consulting Actuary.

1963   Jersey (Channel Isles) Police admitted as members. Sir William Johnson relinquished his post as President. Mr E. J. (later Sir Edward) Dodd appointed President. January – House purchase scheme, linked to Woolwich Building Society began. Death of Mr K.J. Britt.

1964   Sir Herbert Hunter appointed Life Vice President. First PMAS Book Prize awarded to best student at District Police Training Centres.

1965   PMAS became member of National Conference of Friendly Societies. Police Cadets became eligible for membership of PMAS.

1966   Whole Life policies could be surrendered for cash; £2.5 million advanced for mortgages; death of Sir Edward Dodd. Year End – Assets worth nearly £11 million; premiums rose to £1,676,419; investment income reached £584,431

1967   Head Office in Edgbaston extended; Mr A.F. King appointed Deputy Manager & Secretary; Mr F. A. Smith appointed Assistant Secretary; Sir Eric St. Johnston appointed President; Mr P. J. Sharpe and Mr P. R. Woollard appointed to executive. Mr N.A. Horsley retired. Mr K.M. McKelvey appointed Consulting Actuary. Friendly Society limits increased from £500 to £2,500 (or £3,500 if linked to mortgage). Panda Scheme introduced with high death cover for low cost.

1968   Loan scheme introduced. Mr J.R. Furber elected to Committee of Management. Death of Captain S.A. Wood and Sir Herbert Hunter. Mr J. Wright appointed Deputy Chairman.

1969   Extra space required; room rented at No. 7 Greenfield Crescent, Edgbaston as additional office accommodation. Desk computer purchased. Mr E.S. Drake retired as Chairman and appointed Life Vice President. Mr J. Wright appointed Chairman of Committee of Management. Mr J.F. Lumley appointed Deputy Chairman.

1970   Transfer of Head Office to Alexandra House, Lichfield. Official opening of new Registered Office in Lichfield by HRH Princess Alexandra on 24 March. Mr P. R. Woollard resigned. Mr P.H. Crawford appointed Assistant Secretary.

1971   Golden Jubilee Year. Pensioners retiring on ordinary police pensions eligible for membership. January – Unit Trust Endowment Scheme introduced. March – Convertible Option Policy (COP) introduced. June – House purchase scheme introduced, in association with Police Federation. Sir John McKay elected President. Mr P. H. Crawford, Assistant Secretary resigned.

1972   January – Mr J. W. Hadley, Manager & Secretary awarded MBE. Loan scheme phased out. July – Panda scheme discontinued. Mortgage protection policy with/without profits introduced to replace Panda policies. July – Recruits Special Privilege Policy introduced. Alexandra House awarded Lichfield's Civic Society award for the best new building in Lichfield.

1973   NCR Accounting Machine purchased. Temporary loan scheme re-introduced. January – 10 Year Moneyspinner Policy introduced. Death of Mr J.F. Lumley, Deputy Chairman; Mr J.R. Furber appointed Deputy Chairman; Mr P. Simpson appointed Assistant Deputy Chairman. Mr J.M. (later Sir John) Hill appointed President; death of Mr E.S. Drake, Life Vice President.

1974   First presentation of award for Snowdonia Seven competition sponsored by PMAS; Police Powers booklet introduced; micro-filming equipment purchased; Mr J. Wright appointed Life Vice President.

1975   Mr J.W. Hadley retired as Manager & Secretary. July – Mr A. F. King appointed Manager & Secretary; Mr P. J. Sharpe appointed Deputy Manager & Secretary; Mr M.J. Kilgallen appointed Assistant Secretary. October – 15 Year Prosperity Plan introduced; nominations raised to £1,500; recruits limit raised from £500 to £1,000. Year end – new sums assured reached £33,190,718; weekly premiums now £15,248.

1976   Husbands of women police officers eligible as PMAS members. Limits increased to £10,000 per member, with £500 tax exemption. Low Cost Mortgage Endowment Scheme introduced. Mr A.E. Treves appointed a Life Vice President; Sir James Haughton appointed President.

1977   NCR 499 Electronic Data Processing System installed. Mr F.A. Smith, Assistant Manager retired; Mr M. J. Kilgallen appointed Assistant Manager; Mr W. F. Moore appointed Assistant Secretary. Sir Colin Woods appointed President.

1978   July – maximum sum assured increased to £15,500 including £500 tax exemption.

1979   February – death of Mr W. F. Moore, Assistant Secretary; retired members' limit increased to £4,000 Endowment. Mr J. W. D. (later Sir James) Crane appointed President.

1980   Mr J. Wright retired as Chairman. Mr J. R. Furber appointed Chairman of Committee of Management; Mr P. Simpson appointed Deputy Chairman. PMAS Capitaliser Scheme introduced. September – maximum sum assured increased to £25,500. Year end – 19,080 new policies; £98,731,576 sums assured; new annual premiums £2,587,067.

1982　January – Mr A.F. King awarded OBE. March – word processing equipment installed. POLICE 4000 scheme introduced.

1983　January – maximum sum assured increased to £50,500. February – Vax 11/730 computer system installed. Major file conversion from visual to computerised records. April – the Building Society Act introduced MIRAS – Mortgage Interest Relief At Source. Huge increase in mortgage business for PMAS. May – Mr L. (later Sir Lawrence) Byford appointed President. August – computer system went 'live'. October – Mr M. J. Pate appointed Assistant Manager. Year end – 19,074 new policies; £151,263,679 new sums assured

1984　March – tax exemption limit raised to £750; maximum sum assured increased to £60,750; May – nominations increased to £5,000. Miners' Strike resulted in many authorised officers being called for duty on the picket line. September – introduction of Single Premium Investment scheme – Income and Growth Bonds.

1985　First edition of PMAS news-sheet – *Lifeline.* Friendly Society limits on taxable business removed.

1986　May – Mr P. Simpson retired as Deputy Chairman of Committee of Management. Mr B. E. Wallis appointed Deputy Chairman. Mr K. M. McKelvey retired as Consulting Actuary; Mr D. E. A. Sanders took over. Mr W.J. Newton retired as Auditor. July – TOPIC, the Stock Exchange computer terminal installed. October – 'Big Bang', i.e. the de-regulation of the Stockmarket. November – Mr A.F. King retired. Mr P. J. Sharpe appointed Manager & Secretary; Mr M. J. Kilgallen appointed Deputy Manager; Mr M. J. Pate appointed Deputy Secretary; Mr I.V. Dempster appointed Assistant Secretary. Major upgrade of computers combined with purchase of Vax 8200 computer. Enactment of Financial Services Act.

1987   May – new telephone system installed in Head Office, Alexandra House. Mr B. E. Wallis retired as Deputy Chairman of Committee of Management; Mr J. Taylor appointed Deputy Chairman. Mr R.S. (later Sir Richard) Barratt appointed President. September – tax exemption limit changed from £750 sum assured to £100 annual premium. Death of Mr J. Wright, Life Vice President. October – 'Black Monday', the Stockmarket crash.

1988   April – PMAS accepted as member of LAUTRO, the Life Assurance and Unit Trust Regulatory Organisation, to comply with the Financial Services Act, 1986. EC Life Directive implemented, giving wider investment powers but imposing annual actuarial valuations. PMAS membership extended to include civilian members of Head Office staff. August – work commenced on extension to Head Office, Alexandra House.

1989   May – Mr J. R. Furber appointed Life Vice President; PMAS promotional video tape launched. September – Mr A.P. Hunter appointed to executive. Tax exemption fund now £150 per year. Restructuring of PMAS management. Appointment of Fund Managers. Mr L.A. Milner appointed independent non-executive director. December – Alexandra House extension and refurbishment completed.

1990   Discretionary Fund Managers appointed for overseas investments. Change of executive titles – Mr P. J. Sharpe – General Manager; Mr M. J. Kilgallen – Assistant General Manager – Marketing; Mr M. J. Pate – Assistant General Manager – Technical; Mr I. V. Dempster – Assistant General Manager – Operations; Mr A. P. Hunter – Assistant General Manager – Resources. Mr D.S. Parmee appointed Consulting Actuary. Mr J.G. Harris appointed independent non-executive director. A Government Green paper on Friendly Societies created a new framework. March – extension to Alexandra House officially opened by Rt. Hon. Viscount Whitelaw. May – Mr J. Taylor retired as Deputy Chairman; Sir John Woodcock, HM Chief Inspector of Constabulary appointed President. Major upgrading of computer equipment, Vax 4000 system installed. Messrs D. J. Plester and N. G. Pocknell appointed Assistant Chairmen. Mr W. R. Parry appointed Chairman – Accounts Sub-Committee.

1991   Personal computers purchased to replace word processors. May – new PMAS brochure produced; Minimum Low Cost Endowment Policy introduced. Presentation of Armorial Bearings. Society's Award of Merit and President's Certificate of Commendation introduced. First Award of Merit awarded to Mr A. E. (Bert) Treves, Life Vice President. First awards of President's Certificate of Commendation to Messrs W. R. Parry, LL.B, D. J. Plester and N.G. Pocknell. Mr T.G. Arthur appointed independent non-executive director.

1992   Mr A.P. Hunter appointed Chief Accountant. Mr J.P. Parker appointed Assistant General Manager – Resources. Mr W. R. Parry appointed Assistant Chairman following retirement of Mr N. G. Pocknell. Friendly Societies Act 1992 received Royal Assent. Book, The Story of the PMAS published.

A GLOSSARY OF TERMS

ACA	–	Associate of the Institute of Chartered Account-ants
ACC	–	Assistant Chief Constable
ACII	–	Associate of the Chartered Insurance Institute
ACPO	–	Association of Chief Police Officers
AEA	–	Atomic Energy Authority
AGM	–	Annual General Meeting
AIDS	–	Acquired Immune Deficiency Syndrome
AO	–	Authorised Officer
BA	–	Bachelor of Arts
BAAC	–	British Airports Authority Constabulary
BART	–	Baronet (also shown as Bt)
BEM	–	British Empire Medal
BTC	–	British Transport Commission
BIG BANG	–	The name given to the de-regulation of the Stock Exchange in October, 1986
BSc	–	Bachelor of Science
BTP	–	British Transport Police
BLACK MONDAY	–	The Stock Market collapse October 1987
CB	–	Companion of the Order of the Bath
CBE	–	Commander of the Order of the British Empire
CBIM	–	Companion of the British Institute of Manage-ment
CC	–	Chief Constable
CH	–	Companion of Honour
CHIEF HMI	–	Her Majesty's Chief Inspector of Constabulary
CID	–	Criminal Investigation Department

C/INSP	–	Chief Inspector
C/SUPT	–	Chief Superintendent
CMG	–	Companion of the Order of St Michael and St George
COP	–	Convertible Option Policy
CPU	–	Central Planning Unit (for police training)
CVO	–	Commander of the Royal Victorian Order
DCC	–	Deputy Chief Constable
DCI	–	Detective Chief Inspector
DFC	–	Distinguished Flying Cross
D/INSP	–	Detective Inspector
Dip Arch	–	Diploma in Architecture
DL	–	Deputy Lieutenant
D/PC	–	Detective Police Constable
DPTC	–	District Police Training Centre
D/SGT	–	Detective Sergeant
DSO	–	Companion of the Distinguished Service Order
D/SUPT	–	Detective Superintendent
EEC	–	European Economic Community/ Common Market
ENOSIS	–	Cyprus: Union with Greece
EOKA	–	Cyprus: Ethnika Organosis Kypriakou Agonas (National Organisation of Struggle to Unite with Greece)
FCA	–	Fellow of the Institute of Chartered Accountants
FCII	–	Fellow of the Chartered Insurance Institute
FFA	–	Fellow of the Faculty of Actuaries
FIA	–	Fellow of the Institute of Actuaries
HM	–	Her Majesty/His Majesty
HMI	–	Her Majesty's Inspector of Constabulary
HO	–	Home Office
HOLMES	–	Home Office Large Major Incident Enquiry System

Inter alia	–	among other things
INSP	–	Inspector
IRA	–	Irish Republican Army
JP	–	Justice of the Peace
KCVO	–	Knight Commander of the Royal Victorian Order
KPM	–	King's Police Medal
LAPR	–	Life Assurance Premium Relief
LAUTRO	–	Life Assurance and Unit Trust Regulatory Organisation
LLB	–	Bachelor of Laws
LLD	–	Doctor of Laws
£.s.d.	–	Pounds, shillings and pence (pre- decimalisation)
MA	–	Master of Arts
MBE	–	Member of the Order of the British Empire
MC	–	Military Cross
MIAM	–	Member of the Institute of Advanced Motorists
MIPM	–	Member of the Institute of Personnel Management
MIRAS	–	Mortgage Interest Relief at Source
MoD	–	Ministry of Defence
MP	–	Member of Parliament
MVO	–	Member of the Royal Victorian Order
NARPO	–	National Association of Retired Police Officers
OBE	–	Officer of the Order of the British Empire
OStJ	–	Officer of the Order of the Hospital of St John of Jerusalem.
PACE	–	Police and Criminal Evidence Act, 1984
PC	–	Privy Councillor; police constable; personal computer
PF	–	Police Federation of England and Wales
PLA	–	Port of London Authority
PM	–	Prime Minister

PMAA	–	Police Mutual Assurance Association
PMAS	–	Police Mutual Assurance Society
PNC	–	Police National Computer
RIBA	–	Member of the Royal Institute of British Architecture
RUC	–	Royal Ulster Constabulary
QPM	–	Queen's Police Medal
RN	–	Royal Navy
SC	–	Special Constable
SET	–	Selective Employment Tax
SIB	–	Securities and Investments Board
SGT	–	Sergeant
SRO	–	Self-Regulatory Organisation (for life assurance companies and friendly societies)
SUPT	–	Superintendent
TOPIC	–	The name of a computer system which provides up-to-the-minute information on Stock Exchange dealings and share prices
TUC	–	Trades Union Congress/Council
UK	–	United Kingdom
USA	–	United States of America
VAT	–	Value Added Tax
W/PC	–	Woman Police Constable
W/SGT	–	Woman Police Sergeant